TEXTBOOK OF ANTHROPOLOGICAL LINGUISTICS

About the Author

Dr. Kamal Kant Misra has been a Reader in Anthropology at the Central University of Hyderabad since 1989. Between 1978 and 1989 he was a Lecturer in Social Anthropology at Utkas University, Bhubaneswar. He has his anthropological training at Utkas University, Jawaharlal Nehru University and University of Kent at Canterbury. He is a former Gold Medalist of Utkas University for his outstanding performance in M.Sc Examination in Anthropology in 1976.

Dr. Misra's publications include two books, e.g., *Social Structure and Change among the Ho of Orissa* (1987) and *Tribal Elite and Social Transformation* (1994), and about 50 research papers published in journals of repute and in edited volumes.

His main topical interests are, Environment, Culture and Development; Language Culture and Thought; and Theories in Anthropology. South Asia and Pacific are his main regional interests.

TEXTBOOK OF ANTHROPOLOGICAL LINGUISTICS

Kamal K. Misra
Reader in Anthropology
University of Hyderabad, Hyderabad.

CONCEPT PUBLISHING COMPANY, NEW DELHI-110059

ISBN 81-7022-819-0 (H.B.)

First Published 2000

Published and Printed by
Ashok Kumar Mittal
Concept Publishing Company
A/15-16, Commercial Block, Mohan Garden
New Delhi-110059 (India)

Phones: 5648039, 5649024
Fax: 091-(11)-5648053
Email : publishing@conceptpub.com.

Dedicated
to
Nanā and *Bou*
with love and gratitute

PREFACE

From its inception, anthropology as a holistic discipline has been enriching itself by appreciating and articulating the themes of and discourses in other branches of knowledge. The exercise has largely helped anthropological studies to comprehend various dimensions of human culture extensive and objectively. Despite having linkages with many behavioural, natural and social sciences, anthropology has forged an indelible link with linguistics, as language and culture are closely related to each other. Anthropologists have recognized the significance of language not only as a tool for more effective field-work, but as an essential constituent of the cultural fabric which they study. Anthropologists encounter a bewildering variety of speech, which accrue different meanings in different social and cultural contexts. They, therefore, look at language not from the point of view of philology or psychology and philosophy, but from social and cultural dimensions. This relationship between language and culture was apparently recognized by Franz Boas a little less than a century ago, which is being resurrected from time to time in the writings of Sapir, Bloomfield, Lévi-Strauss, Dell Hymes, among others. Because of this social and cultural emphases in the study of language, anthropology curriculum all over the world invariably includes basic orientation in linguistics for its students. Many University Departments in Anthropology in India also impart training in anthropological linguistics as an elective course to the students specializing in social and cultural anthropology. These students most often feel and need of a textbook on the subject for their personal use, which should be handy and affordable. This book is a modest attempt in this direction. A specialist reader or an advanced student in the subject may find the contents of this book sketchy and discussions brief, and hence, I must confess that neither this book is exhaustive and elaborate nor is it even intended to be; it is rather designed to fulfil the limited objective of initiating the students into the subject.

My experience as a University teacher for more than 20 years is that anthropology is not being taught at the under-graduate level in many states of India. Therefore, the students of M.A./M.Sc. in anthropology come from various non-anthropology backgrounds. Even in the states where the under-graduate curriculum includes anthropology honours or pass, Linguistic Anthropology does not always constitute a part of the courses of study. As a result, when the students have to undergo training in Linguistic Anthropology, they invariably encounter initial problems in comprehending the subject. Keeping this in view, this book is written with the aim that it caters best to the needs of such beginners of the subject.

This book could not have been completed, but for the help and encouragement of many individuals and institutions. I am grateful to many batches of my students, whose insistence to write a book on the subject prompted me to collect and organize my class notes into a book form. I am very much grateful to them. The University Grants Commission, New Delhi deserves my thanks for encouraging me to write this book by extending financial support under its university level textbook writing programme. I am also thankful to the Commonwealth Scholarship Commission in the U.K., London, for offering me a visiting fellowship in 1996-97, during which the final chapters of the book were written. I am thankful to the Department of Anthropology, University of Kent at Canterbury, United Kingdom, for providing me all possible facilities for the completion of the book there. Mr. Alan Bicker, Dr. Peter Parkes, Dr. Michael Fisher, Dr. Kristin Kocher, Mrs. Jan Horn and others at the University of Kent at Canterbury, United Kingdom deserve my thanks for extending a warm academic atmosphere to me during my one year stay there. I am also thankful to the University of Hyderabad, and particularly, its Department of Anthropology and my colleagues there, who had ungrudgingly shared my work-load in my absence and allowed me to complete this work.

I cannot sufficiently express my gratitude to Professor Roy Ellen, Head of the Department of Anthropology, University of Kent at Canterbury, for his intellectual stimuli, and for having gone through all the chapters of the book and offering many constructive suggestions for its improvement. Needless to say, and lapse is exclusively mine. I am also thankful to Miss Joan White for her compassion, understanding and encouragement that helped me to concentrate on this book during my stay at Canterbury. I am grateful to Miss Nancy White, Mr. Ben Rowden, Miss Lilian Smith, the Nolans, Mrs. Holland, Paddy, Di and their kids, and many other friends for their friendly support.

Sushma, Riki and Ritu have always been cooperative and considerate, and they are the inspirations to all my academic ventures. I am indeed grateful to them. I am thankful to M/s Concept Publishing Company, New Delhi for their support and enthusiasm in publishing this book. I am greatly inspired by the silent sacrifices of my parents, and it is impossible to repay the debt except dedicating this book to them.

Hyderabad Central University, **Kamal K. Misra**
14 July 1999.

CONTENTS

LIST OF FIGURES

LIST OF TABLES

1

LINGUISTICS, ANTHROPOLOGY AND OTHER SCIENCES

Linguistics, its meaning and scope

The simplest definition of linguistics perhaps is that it is 'the scientific study of language'. Since language is an integral part of culture, any study of culture essentially involves the study of language. But it is evident that the study of language is a herculean responsibility because of the existence of a large number of languages all over the world. A very moderate estimate puts the number of languages as over five thousand. But, in reality, every language has a number of *dialects* arising from local peculiarities of vocabulary, pronunciation, and idiom, and spoken in different geographical regions within the same linguistic zone. Sometimes, the dialects of the same language are so different that these appear to be distinct languages themselves. Further, every individual has a very special way of speaking the language, differing in some details from that of other speakers of the same dialect or language, which is commonly known as the *idiolect;* and hence, it is said, any language has as many idiolects as the number of its speakers. Furthermore, an individual possesses several idiolects, as he is supposed to use a particular style of language at specific places and on specific occasions. For example, he does not use the same language of address to his seniors, to his contemporaries and to his younger siblings. Similarly, he does not use the same language in temples or churches, class-rooms, public places and at home. From all these considerations, the study of language needs the skill and motivation of the linguist, who attempts to study language in a systematic fashion. Linguistics, therefore, dwells upon the following questions: what is the nature of language?, what is its structure and what are its functions?, what are the similarities and differences between various languages?, how it originated and evolved? how is it unique to *Homo sapiens sapiens?*, how is it acquired and transmitted?, how it takes different forms in different cultural and social settings?, how does it change? and so on. From an anthropological point of view, all these questions assume importance as they are related to the process of origin and evolution of man as a biological and as a cultural being.

Nature of Human Language

The question now arises as to what is a language? In order to understand it, let us not go for a definition, although there are so many of them. Let us first know, what is the nature of language? Perhaps, the first and the foremost characteristic of language is that it is **human**. In fact, researches on animal behaviour do indicate that non-human animals, birds and insects have some form of language, in the sense that they are capable of communicating among each other. For example, experiments have been conducted on chimpanzees, horses, dolphins, bees, ants etc. to probe into their respective ways of communication. But it is unique for man to have a language with enormous varieties, enabling him to communicate with so ease and sophistication. It is, therefore, said that man uses sound signals which are distinct from other animals.

The other characteristic of human language is its **arbitrariness**. This means that there is no obvious connection between the signal and the message in human language. For example, why a horse has been called a horse and not a dog has no answer to our satisfaction. It may be seen that almost all the words that we use in our everyday life to denote so many things are just arbitrary. However, there are certain exceptions to this. In many languages, there are some *onomatopoeic* sounds. The *onomatopoeic* sounds are supposed to be directly derived from the nature and adopted by man in course of time. For example, words like *bang, quack-quack, ding-dong* etc. are the natural sounds incorporated into the language.

Human language occupies a distinct place in the domain of animal communication because it has to be **learned**. While the communication between other animals and birds is mostly genetically in-built instincts, it is different among the human beings. The communication among the honey-bees or among the cows, for example, is the one which needs no training for them. But in case of man, language training is a prolonged process; during the childhood and with the growing age, the human child acquires the language skill. In fact, the family around the child plays an instrumental role in the teaching process by encouraging while the child uses the right signals and rectifying the wrong ones. The child internalises all the required right signals gradually as a part of the language training process. This also speaks about the transmissibility of the human language from generation to generation, which is not found among other animals, birds or insects.

Unlike non-human modes of communication, human language demonstrates a structural difference. It is invariably organised into two layers of sounds. This nature of human language is most commonly known as **duality** or **double articulation**. Let us try to understand this phenomenon. Researches have revealed that different non-human species use vocal signals for the purpose of communication. For example, a cow uses less than ten signals, dolphins and gorillas have between twenty and thirty etc. The fact remains that all these animals use each basic sound only once to communicate something without combining these sounds with some other sounds. Of course, the non-human animals can repeat the same sound for similar message. The unique thing with man is that he can combine these sounds to make a large number of meaningful units from a small number of sounds for multifarious expression of ideas and sentiments. An example may help to explain this more clearly. Man is capable of producing between thirty and forty basic sounds or *phonemes*, which are not numerically very high compared to other animals. Each *phoneme* in itself is meaningless, but can be combined with some other specific *phonemes* to produce many meaningful words with much ease for communication. For example, sounds such as *f, d, g, o,* mean nothing separately. But when combined differently among themselves, *fog, dog, god* are produced for communicating different things. It may be noted that duality or double articulation in human language makes it more flexible, in the sense that greater number of messages can be sent with this process than the one without it.

Human language is distinct among all kinds of animal communication, because of its characteristic **displacement**. This means that the human language is capable of expressing present events as efficiently as the events of the past or future. To put it differently, the human language can refer to the things that are absent as perfectly as the things that are present. But what happens in case of a dog or a cat? The animal produces a sound indicating the presence of an enemy, when the enemy is actually present. On the other hand, it does not produce such a sound under a normal condition. The human capability of producing any kind of sound under any circumstance accelerates his capacity to communicate a wide range of information at any time without any difficulty.

Many experiments on non-human communication have revealed that no animal other than man can create or produce new utterances or new sounds whenever necessary. This quality of human language is essentially known as **creativity** or **productivity**. On the other hand, most of the other kinds of animal communication is monotonous and stereotyped. Many of these messages are instinctual like intention of having food or sex, need for a shelter or protection etc. Humans, therefore, are uniquely endowed with a capability of creating new vocal means of communication, which we do not find among other animals.

Among all the animal modes of communication, it is the human language, which is highly rule governed or **patterned**. In case of other animals, the communication is simply based on a set of elements that are repeated, if necessary. A dog, for example, keeps on barking in a given way until the threat is out of sight. But in the case of human language, sounds are arranged in such a systematic manner that these convey a definite message very clearly and unambiguously. The combination between different sound units or phonemes follows a most rigorous pattern and cannot just be put together as a haphazard heap of individual sounds.

If we put together all these characteristics, it becomes easier to define language. Language, then, is a patterned system of arbitrary sound signals, characterised by creativity, displacement, duality, which is learned and culturally transmitted from one generation to the next.

Although we find a large number of languages which are apparently quite dissimilar, their main characteristics outlined above are the same. Therefore, there is no language in the world which might be called inferior or more primitive to any other language. The principle of *cultural relativism* also applies to language, and hence, we might as well speak of *linguistic relativism* to understand the relationship between languages. The people of the technologically simpler societies might not be using all the words that their neighbours use, but that does not handicap them to express themselves as efficiently as we do in our own language. Moreover, since the underlying structure of all languages has many things in common, Santali or Gondi is as complex as English or German.

Branches of Linguistics

Depending upon one's vantage point, linguistics could be divided in a number of ways. For example, it can be divided into the kinds of languages that are spoken in different geographical areas of the world. Therefore, we have linguists specialising in *Indo-European* linguistics, *American-Indian* linguistics etc. In fact, these major language families are further subdivided into many smaller languages, which come under the purview of analysis by specialist linguists.

If linguistics is the study of language in its entirety, including the temporal and spatial dimensions, there are at least two ways of studying it, eventually dividing linguistics into two major branches. The first branch is known as **descriptive** linguistics and the second one as **historical** or **comparative** linguistics. Descriptive linguistics is basically a synchronic study of the structure of a language at a given point of time. Mostly it looks at the internal pattern of a language rather than its historical linkages. On the other hand, historical or comparative linguistics describes changes in language systems over a period of time. Its scope also includes the study of familial or genealogical relationships between different languages, or that of the branches of a language. A special branch of linguistics which involves both synchronic (descriptive) and diachronic (historical) approaches is known as **linguistic geography**, which aims at studying the spatial diffusion patterns of a language or a language system. The relationship between linguistics and other sister sciences has created further branches in linguistics, which we shall consider below.

Linguistics and Anthropology

Anthropology has claimed a special status among all the branches of social sciences because of its emphasis on holistic study of man. If holism is understood in its right spirit, one cannot deny the role of linguistics in anthropological study of man. In fact, the anthropological vision of man is enriched by the study of its biology, prehistory, ethnology and language. Hence, study of language has been an integral part of anthropology, both in teaching and in research.

The operational necessity of linguistic training in anthropological research has been expressed in no uncertain terms by Sapir, as is evident from his remark : "Some day the attempt to master a primitive culture without the help of the language of its society will seem as amateurish as the labours of a historian who cannot handle the original documents of the civilisations which he is describing" (Mandelbaum, 1949 : 162).

The study of language within the context of anthropology and the inevitable overlap between the studies of language and culture have been long recognised by the fathers of the discipline of anthropology, which has been known as *Ethnolinguistics*. For example, in Britain, Sir Edward Tylor's *Primitive Culture* (1871) and *Anthropology* (1881), Marett's *Anthropology* (1912), Malinowski's *Coral Garden and Their Magic* (1935) began with the conviction that language and culture need an integral study, particularly in case of the simple societies of the world. Later, however, other British scholars like Hocart, Haddon, Gardiner, J.R. Firth, Robins, Nadel, Evans-Pritchard and many others strengthened this foundation. In this tradition, language and other aspects of culture are conceptualised as the interdependence of different aspects of the same event or social action (Hymes, 1964 : 5).

Not only in Britain, but also in France, there was an intellectual upsurge during the early decades of this century, which prioritised the study of the relations between language and culture. It was believed by the great thinkers of the time that language is primarily a shared, socially inherited system (Hymes : *ibid*). In fact, this relationship between language and society led de Saussure, the founder of structural linguistics, to distinguish between *la langue* and *la parole.* While, for de Saussure, the former pertained to the linguistic system of the society and its collective norm, the latter related to the individual person and event. Along with de Saussure, Meillet, Durkheim and Mauss maintained the position that language was very much a social phenomenon and was subjected to the same analysis as other social events. The most outstanding contribution from France, however, came from Claude Lévi-Strauss during the middle of this century in the form of structuralism in anthropology, which emphasised that like linguistic phenomena, social phenomena were the facets of a single underlying factor, and that was the mind. Hence, they were subjected to similar line of analysis.

The history of relations between the studies of language and culture in the United States is indeed very old. Although the recognition of the relationship between language and culture may be traced to the writings of Jefferson and Thoreau, the single most outstanding contribution to the study of linguistic anthropology came from Franz Boas during the first quarter of this century. Boas, Kroeber, Sapir, Pike, Bloomfield and many others continued their interest in the study of language as an anthropological exercise with the rejection of mentalism and reinforcing the descriptive method. That is why, linguistics in the United States is often associated with the label of descriptivism. The study of language and world view by Sapir and Whorf and the emergence of cognitive anthropology during the middle of this century, connecting language with cultural analysis, consolidated into new areas of *ethnolinguistics*. Studies on the native perception of colour, diseases, kinship etc. opened up a new dimension to the understanding of culture with the help of language.

If language is accepted as a social and/or cultural phenomenon, which is in fact already accepted by the scholars, there is no room to doubt the relationship between anthropology and linguistics. Despite having various theoretical differences, anthropologists and linguists admittedly depend upon each other, as an anthropologist needs the help of linguistic models for the best understanding of his data and a linguist needs the ethnographic details for the formulation of his models. Boas, therefore, aptly remarked, "Whatever our literary and artistic or our philosophical and religious grasp of human ways, the scientific understanding of man will in all likelihood grow from our understanding of language...." (Boas, 1939 : 105-106).

Language and its analysis are also closely connected with physical or biological anthropology as much as to social and cultural anthropology. Physical anthropology demonstrates as to how physiological adaptation during the process of hominisation has eventually made man capable of speaking. Besides this, there are even suggestions that genetics may have a bearing on speech production and speech variation. During the early decades of this century, studies by Van Ginneken, for exmaple, suggested that divergent phonetic systems in different subcultures might be accounted for by hereditary factors. Studies by Luchsinger (1940) and Tarnoczy (1947) are said to have established the genetic basis for individual differences in the articulatory mechanism. Darlington (1947) in a controversial study has attempted to show the correlation between the frequency of genes in 'O' blood group and the presence of 'th' and 'dh' sounds in a culture. In fact, Darlington assumed that the genetic factors could make for increased ease or difficulty in the articulation of certain phonetic elements among the speakers in a given culture. However remote it might appear to be, physical anthropology has also a close link with linguistics and many overlapping areas of research interest.

The third main branch of anthropology, prehistoric archaeology, facilitates the study of historical linguistics or comparative philology to a considerable extent. The associated finds from an excavated site by an archaeologist, particularly the symbolic artifacts, when decoded, could throw light on the culture of the prehistoric civilisations. For example, the seals excavated from Mohenjo-daro and Harappa and the writings on them could speak many hitherto unknown things about the culture, once it is properly decoded. However, an archaeological find may be used to study the trees of language of the world. On the other hand, language provides authentic evidence for the reconstruction of cultural history of civilisations and the processes of diffusion and integration. The overlap of methods between prehistoric archaeology and linguistics has been emphasised in more recent times. Like the prehistorians' C^{14} method of dating to suggest the age of the artifacts, the linguists have been preoccupied with glottochronology and lexicostatistical techniques to suggest the age at which two or more languages got separated from a common stock.

Linguistics and Sociology

Sociolinguistics is the branch of linguistics which concentrates on the examination of how and why people use language as they interact with other members of their society. In considering any spoken communication, one can notice that a speaker's language reveals information on his sex, approximate age, regional and ethnic origins, education, profession and attitude to his listeners. Language variation in a social context is also a part of the field of sociolinguistics. G.H. Mead in the book, *Mind, Self and Society* (1934) has emphasised the role of language as a means of social control in developing a consciousness of the 'other' through a process of verbal role playing. It is however true that either man selects the language at every social situation, or the social condition creates an opportunity for him to use a given type of language. Apart from this, variations in gender, age, caste, class, status, ethnicity, education, occupation or profession and other social situations culminate in very definite linguistic variations, which constitute the scope of sociolinguistics. As all communities are not monolingual, sociolinguistics also addresses to language use in bilingual and multilingual communities. In multilingual communities, lingua francas have often grown up as a means of communication, and a sociolinguist studies the similarities in the nature of the lingua francas in different parts of the world. Sociolinguists thus set themselves the task of examining language use, its variation, its development, change and standardisation, its regional and class dialects, its lingua francas, its specialised codes and so on. The scope of sociolinguistics is by no means confined to the study of language in its social context mostly as a static phenomenon, but also as a dynamic process. The process of social mobility has also its inevitable impact on the language of the person or the group, which sociolinguistics also very well brings to its fold for discussion.

Linguistics and Psychology

Linguistics is as much about mental behaviour as it is about social behaviour. This explains the intimate relationship between linguistics and psychology. The psychological way of understanding language has opened up an established subfield of linguistics, known as *psycholinguistics*. This branch deals with the relationship between language and mind, focusing mainly on how language is learnt, stored and occasionally lost. In fact, we can divide this relationship into two aspects: acquisition and performance, and the two are interlinked. Acquiring is the ability to perform, that is, to use language with appropriateness, and performance is essential to complete the process of acquisition. Psychological explanations appear in many facets of linguistics, such as, in the origin and development of language, individual differences in language behaviour, speech pathology, acquisition of first and subsequent languages, language and thought and so on. What is remarkable is the ability of the human child to acquire and master the intricacies of the language in an incredibly short span of time. This phenomenon of language learning has been theorised either as 'behaviourism' by Skinner or as 'mentalism' by others, about which we shall discuss more in subsequent chapters. Psycholinguists also attempt to understand dysphasia (bad speech), dyslexia (word blindness) and aphasia (sudden or gradual loss of language for many reasons) etc. Although psycholinguistics has tried to throw some light on the mystery of human linguistic ability, every time researchers realise how little they know about the mystery of human language and how much more research is needed to understand it completely.

Linguistics and Philosophy

There are certain vexing problems of philosophy which are closely related to linguistics, and one of them is *epistemology*, which has made philosophers look to language. *Epistemology* is concerned with the nature and validity of knowledge. Because language plays a large part in the statements we make about the world as we view it, it is understandable to find that the signs and symbols used in language play a major role in epistemological discussions. In their search for meaning, philosophers and linguists invariably look at *syntactics*, thus integrating the interests of both the disciplines.

Linguistics and Neuro-physiology

It has been already said in this chapter that the human child is the only one among all the animals, which learns and uses his language or the *mother tongue*, but without being deliberately taught. The question that therefore comes to our mind is : what neurological features in man explain this unique ability? Further, how is the human brain different from that of other animals, and how did it develop to enable speech, listening, memory and recapitulation? In general, the study of all these problems constitute the domain of *neurolinguistics*. In this field also, linguists share a common research platform with neuro-physiologists and neuro-surgeons.

Applied Linguistics

Recently, the insights gained in sociolinguistics and psycholinguistics have been applied to language teaching and learning, which have opened up a new field in linguistics, known as *applied linguistics*. Although it has been established that any human language is capable of being translated into any other, mere word-for-word translation is inadequate to understand the intricacies of meaning of a different language. On the contrary, what is necessary is the native speaker's innate knowledge, as he uses the language differently, depending upon the subject matter and the audience. Keeping this in mind, courses in English for Special Purposes (ESP) are devised to help the non-English speakers to acquire English. Some methods have been proposed to make the second language acquisition easier, which we shall discuss in detail in appropriate sections.

Linguistics is now closely associated with other fields of knowledge like culture history in the historical reconstruction of cultures, with education in the matter of language teaching, with computer science in the areas of artificial intelligence and computational linguistics, with literature in the field of stylistics and so on. Therefore, with the expansion of human knowledge, linguistics is also extending its academic horizon to understand holistically the uniqueness of man as a language producer and user.

2

LANGUAGE ORIGIN, EVOLUTION, ACQUISITION AND DEVELOPMENT OF WRITING

ORIGIN OF LANGUAGE

In this chapter, we shall deal with the origin of human language, the relationship between language and biological evolution, acquisition of language and development of writing. Before we consider the origin of human language, we should remember that the views expressed in this context are highly conjectural and speculative. The reason, however, is very simple. Anthropologists are of the opinion that *Homo erectus* existed at least one million years from now. From a very rough estimate, it is presumed, the transformation from *erectus* to *sapiens* occurred around 500,000 years ago, and *Homo sapiens sapiens* came into being around 50,000 years ago. But the evidence of the earliest written records is hardly six thousand years old, dating back to the writings of the ancient Sumerians about 4000 B.C. From such a recent record, it is impossible to hypothesise in any concrete terms about the origin of human language. However, we shall critically examine some of the theories and evidences.

The Divine Theory

This theory attributes the origin of language to divine sources, as told by the saints and myth-makers, and believed by the common man. According to Judeo-Christian beliefs and in the biblical account of the creation of the world, we find that the original language was used by Adam while speaking to God in His language. Then, of course, the *original* language was spoken by Adam and

Eve and their descendants until the time of the building of the Tower of Babel. In ancient Egypt, it was believed that the creator of speech was the god Thoth, while for the ancient Babylonians, the language giver was the god Nabu. Similarly, the Hindus believe that although the universe was created by the god Bramha, it was mother Saraswati who spoke the first language and gave it to man. Many simple societies all over the world have their own mythical beliefs about the origin of language. Taking all these views together, we may conclude that at the present, there is no way either to support or to discard any of these propositions, as we cannot either prove or disprove the existence of God, which is a domain of purely individual belief.

Natural Sound or 'Bow-wow' Theory

The **natural sound** or what is commonly known as the 'bow-wow' theory sees the human habit of imitating natural sounds as the beginning of human language. There is no doubt that there are quite a few *onomatopoeic* sounds that have found their-way into the human language. We can take the examples of *bow-wow, meow, crash, boom, cuckoo, crack, purr, whiz, hum, caw, croak, chatter* and many others is support of the theory.

Another variant of the natural sound theory is the **ouch theory**, which suggests that natural instinctive cries or emotive sounds have become transformed into language in the course of time. The human ejaculation of fear, pain, surprise, pleasure, anger and so on became a part of the language. Jean Jacques Rousseau in the middle of the 18th century and Charles Darwin in the late 19th century shared the view about the continuity between the animal and human means of communication taking into account these natural cries.

Both these propositions outlined above have some validity, except the fact that the number of onomatopoeic or natural cry sounds in any given language is so small that it is very difficult to believe that language has evolved from either of them. Again, it is held that as words alone do not constitute a language, these hypotheses are insufficient to explain language origins.

Gestural Language Theory

In an article published in 1976, Hewes has suggested that the use of body parts for communication might have preceded the vocal language in case of the humans. In fact, even now despite an immense sophistication of our vocal language, we also use our body organs sometimes as a means of communication along with the vocal language. The expression of joy and happiness or anger or frustration or an achievement or victory takes a simultaneous form of oral and gestural expressions. Therefore, Hewes' claim cannot be absolutely unfounded. But the only objection to this suggestion could be that there is no evidence of the *time* and *need* for such a shift from gestural language to a vocal language. when we overwhelmingly use vocal language, only with a lesser frequency of gestural language.

Functional Theory

The necessity of language to coordinate certain common group tasks is sometimes said to be the reason for the origin of human language. This idea goes by the name of the functional theory of the origin of human language. The main emphasis here is that language facilitates communication while performing the communal activities. Therefore, when man first started living in a group and shared group tasks, language gradually started evolving. The main objection to this theory is that a vocal language is not essential to carry out group work, which could as well be performed even with a gestural or sign language. Further, the evolutionary relationship between group work and a communication system as complex as that of human language is weak, because the more powerful and expressive language cannot be accounted for by the need for communicating during collective action.

When all the above postulations are apparently not convincing to suggest a scientifically sound theory of the origin of human language, it is plausible that the biological evolution of man might throw some light on it. Therefore, most often linguists look at the process of human evolution, more particularly, the physiology and anatomy of the human body and the changes in its brain size, to look for an explanation to its capability to speak. In the following section, we shall deal with language and biological evolution of man in search of a relatively convincing explanation.

LANGUAGE AND BIOLOGICAL EVOLUTION

In the words of an eminent biologist, George G. Simpson, language is the ". . . . most entirely unique, the most completely diagnostic characteristic of *Homo sapiens*" (1969). From his point of view, language is part of the biological heritage of mankind and is functionally connected with the process of hominisation.

When Charles Darwin published the *Origin of Species* in 1855, he was criticized for not paying much attention to the evolution of man's higher mental faculties and the capability of speech making. Precisely for this reason, Darwin devoted considerable attention to the problem of speech in his later book, *Descent of Man*. He wrote that the mental powers of man might have developed in some early progenitor. The continued advancement of the mental power would have reacted on the mind to empower him to have long process of thought. This complex thought process might not have been pursued without the aid of words (Hammond, 1966: 45). Darwin's hypothesis was, therefore, to look for the presence of speech in man in the process of hominid evolution.

The understanding of the evolution of man's capacity for language must entail an inquiry into a physiological cerebral mechanism as well as certain peripheral instrumentalities to fulfil the task of coordinating between the lips, palate, tongue, pharynx, larynx, and respiratory apparatus. It is not that some of the non-human apes do not possess any of these, but man is specially endowed with all these features together to become the only species to produce language spontaneously in the whole of the animal kingdom.

The first of man's known ancestors to have a culture and possibly some form of language comes from South and East Africa and belongs to the *Australopithecine* subfamily of the *Hominidae* family. It is more than 2 million years old. Australopithecines are characterised by an upright posture and the capacity to use simple tools. **Upright** or **erect posture** has brought about many anatomical changes in man and has became a turning point in the history of human evolution.

The changes in the lower skeleton, especially the pelvis, the lumbar region of the spinal column, the proximal and the distal ends of the femur, and the nature and orientation of the occiput very well prove that the australopithecine was well adapted to upright posture and hence, bipedal locomotion. The upright posture must have made him free to prepare and use tools with greater ease. However, it is suggested that tool use is both the cause and effect of hominid bipedalism, and the evolution of erect posture occurred simultaneously with earliest use of tools.

Erect posture in Australopithecine led to some more anatomical developments that were of remarkable significance in man's biological adaptation for speaking. Because of having an upright posture, the **pharynx** became enlarged, elongated and bent, compared to the quadrupeds, where it is suspended at the end of the spinal column. The pharynx, is a part of the vocal tract between the back of the tongue and the larynx. The enlarged pharynx acted as an important **resonator** used in the production of speech sounds.

The process of hominisation is also characterised by the very significant dental reduction in man, compared to the pre-hominids. Among the australopithecine, there is a definite evidence of reduction of the whole canine-premolar complex, closely comparable to the typical human condition. But the molar still remained large and was primitive in morphology. However, the trend of reduction in molar dentition began since the middle pleistocene and continued throughout the remaining period of the epoch. Associated with dental reduction, Darwin suggests, human evolution is marked by the size of facial skeleton and masticatory muscles. In fact, because of the changes in the anatomy of the human jaw and reduction in the size of the teeth, the **mouth cavity** or **oral chamber** in man evolved as a second resonator for the production of speech sounds. The small and flexible **tongue** in man was an added advantage, as it could move freely inside and at the periphery of the oral chamber

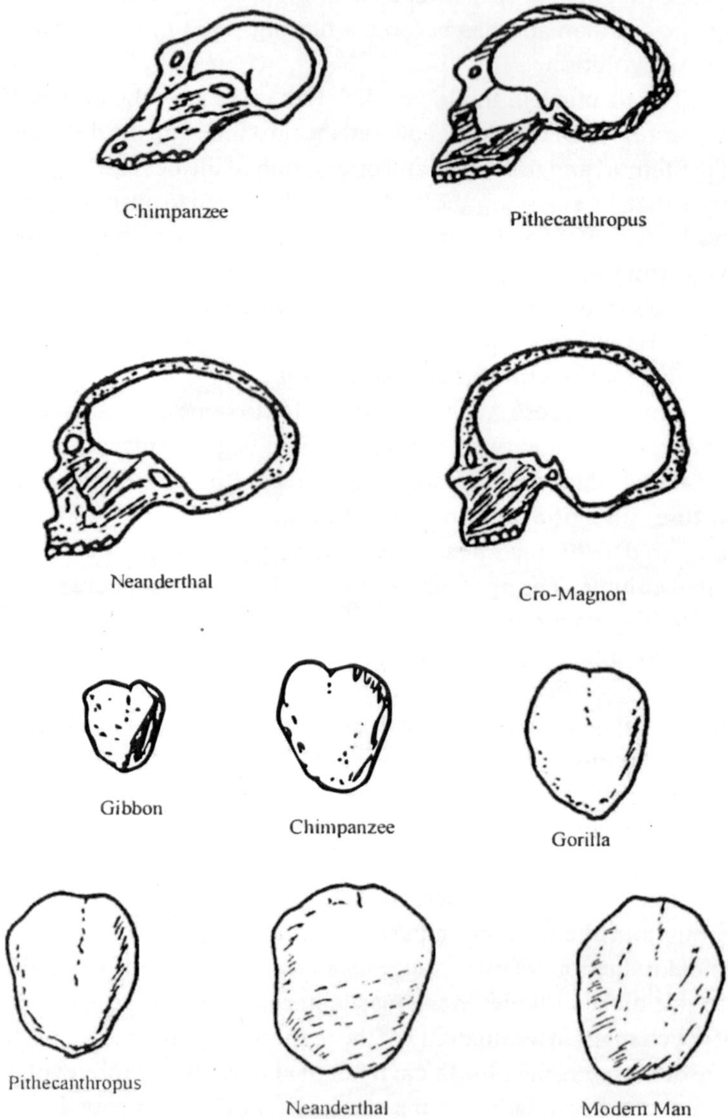

FIG. 2.1 : Comparison of Brain Size of Anthropoids and Man

in articulating speech sounds. The **nasal cavity** in man constituted the third resonator for the production of a variety of speech sounds without any difficulty.

The evolution of language is also very closely associated with the increase in the size and complexity of the human brain. As we shall see from the following Table 2.1, the **cranial capacity** has increased almost four-fold in the course of approximately 2 million years of human history. When the average cranial capacity of a chimpanzee is between 350 and 450 cc, it has gone up to 1200 to 1500 cc in case of *Homo sapiens*. The enlargement of the cranial capacity is naturally associated with increased human intelligence; and therefore, language and human intelligence are two aspects of the same evolutionary development.

TABLE 2.1: **Cranial Capacity in Chimpanzee and Man**

Species	*Size in cc*
Homo sapiens	1200 - 1500
Java and Pekin man (*Homo erectus*)	900 - 1100
Australopithecines	400 - 550
Chimpanzee	350 - 450

Source: After Hammond (1966); 23.

The enlargement of the cranium was not just enough for man to acquire the ability to speak. The cranial capacity was also associated with the expansion of various parts of the human brain. There is an enlargement of the occipital lobes, which are associated with vision. There is also a strong development of the temporal lobes, responsible for visual and auditory stimuli and for recall and reactivation of past experiences. The frontal lobes are also enlarged under the high, bulging forehead with folded and convoluted cortex or surface portion containing motor and sensory areas, which are associated with the movement of the fingers, the hand and the mouth. But it may be noted that these developments are not unique for man, as he shares these features with most of the higher primates. For a long time, however, it was presumed that the asymmetrical development of the human brain with unequal development of the left and right hemispheres was probably very special to man. Hence, **lateralization** was thought to be unique to humans, as certain surface areas were highly developed to enable man to have speech, word memory and associations. Recent evidences however show that, both anatomically and functionally, canaries and zebra finches display lateralization of function, thus further complicating the hypothesis that lateralization was alone responsible for the development of speech in man (Fromkin and Rodman, 1978: 31).

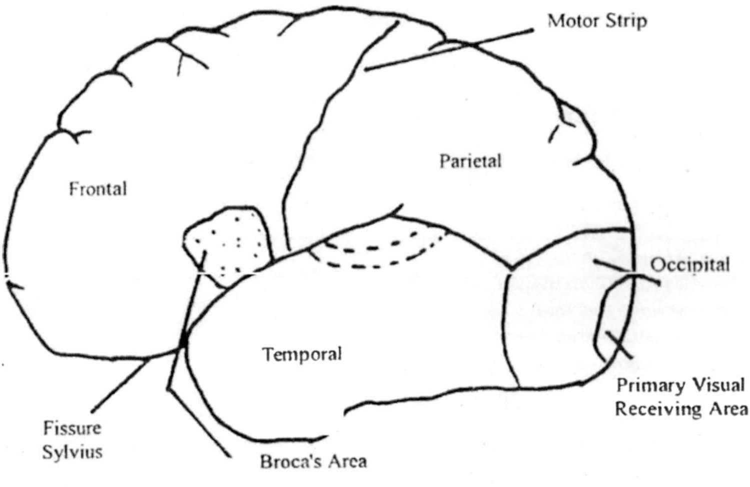

FIG.2.2 : Left Cerebral Hemisphere

Neurological studies have, therefore, revealed that all parts of the human brain are not responsible for all kinds of functions. On the other hand, there are specialised areas that perform special functions. In 1861, a French surgeon and anatomist, Paul Broca reported that a small area in the posterior inferior part of the frontal lobe in the **left** cerebral hemisphere of the human brain was responsible for speech. This area is popularly known as **Broca's area**. In 1865, Broca claimed that speech and other functions of the human brain were highly localised, and if the specific part was not affected, it did not handicap man in performing his regular functions. This theory of **speech localization** claims that while damage to the left cerebral hemisphere produces a condition of **aphasia**, which is a broad term encompassing numerous syndromes of communicative impairment, damage to the right hemisphere leaves the linguistic capability of man almost intact.

Social Factors in Language Evolution

Although biological evolution and eventual anatomical and physiological changes in man must have set the basis of his ability to speak, biologists and physical anthropologists never undermine the role of many social factors in the evolution of language. The foremost social factor considered in this regard is the human habit of **communal living**. Biologists realise that communal living is an important factor in survival, which can be traced among the lower species of the animal kingdom. However, in the higher ranks of Mammalia, there is greater coordination of group activity, which might ultimately have necessitated the use of speech among men. Lord Monboddo, for example, opined that society came first and perhaps existed for ages before language developed, for man is by nature a political as well as a speaking animal. Among others, Revesz has proposed that 'contact reactions' or the basic, innate tendency of social animals to approach one another, establish rapport cooperate and communicate etc. are necessary preconditions of linguistic communication. Grace de Laguna has also stressed that the progressively elaborate communal life in man synchronised with the development of speech, as planned hunting forays, the need for securing safety by night, the indoctrination of the young and related activities must have been considerably assisted by the faculty of speech. Therefore, going by the archaeological record, by the middle of the palaeolithic age, roughly about 1,00,000 years B.P, when man was living in caves or in open camps in groups, he must have been speaking some kind of language to coordinate many of the group activities outlined above.

Allied to the notion of communal living is the role of **manufacturing and increasing utilisation of tools**, as an immediate precursor of speech. Tool using like picking up a piece of sharp stone, a stick, a shell etc. and using it as a weapon straightaway to kill a game, which are in no way inconsistent with the primate behaviour in general, do not necessarily mean the acquisition of speech. But when man started breaking a stick into two pieces or pulling it out of a bush and keeping it aside for future use, the first beginning of speech might have been possible. Further, with the making of the flake tools or acquaintance with the art of retouching a tool for finer uses, he might be using speech of some kind, as by this time man had started perceiving and thinking, and was bestowed with some degree of innovativeness.

Closely linked with the establishment of a communal living and manufacture and use of tools, delegation of **labour** can also be reckoned as a factor in the evolution of speech. With communal living and tool making, human labour emerged as a new form of social activity, which possibly provoked man to use speech. In fact, the Soviet neurologist, Seppe, proposed that work was the main factor in the development of higher, abstract thinking and speech of man. In a significant note Stalin observed, "In the history of mankind, a spoken language has been one of the forces which helped human beings to emerge from the animal world, unite into communities, develop their faculty of thinking, organise social production, wage a successful struggle against the forces of nature, and attain the stage of progress we have today" (Hammond, 1966: 51).

Neanderthal as the Speaking Hominid

Although the evidence of a speaking hominid goes back to about 2 million years with the attempt to prove that australopithecus was capable of speaking, some experimentation has been done to establish that the vocal tract of Neanderthal was very much suitable for speech production. Philip Lieberman and E.S. Crelin have attempted in this direction and have reconstructed the Neanderthal vocal tract from two available complete fossil skulls and a mandible. They have compared the skulls of the newborn human child with that of the reconstructed Neanderthal and have proved that about 75,000 years back, the Neanderthal was capable of speaking.

Lieberman and Crelin have found that both the skulls have many features in common. For example, both are relatively elongated from front to back and flattened from top to bottom. The lower jaw or the mandible is similar in shape in both the skulls with the chin development lacking. Further, seen from below, the dental arch in both the skulls is U-shaped and not V-shaped as in case of adult human beings. From these and other features, the authors have concluded that "the skeletal features of Neanderthal man show that his supralaryngeal vocal apparatus was similar to that of a newborn human infant" (quoted in Hickerson, 1980: 14). But because of high location of the larynx, they suggested, the Neanderthal was incapable of producing the whole range of sounds that a modern man produced. The controversial exercise however concluded that Neanderthal man "was not as well-equipped for language as modern man, but represents an intermediate stage in the evolution of language" (*ibid*: 16).

Lessons from Primate Communicative Behaviour

We have seen in the last Section that the human brain has a lot in common with other arboreal and ground dwelling primates. Naturally, then, it is speculated that the anthropoid apes, evolutionarily closer to man, like the gorillas and the chimpanzees also have some capability to understand and communicate through language. In order to prove this, some very interesting experimental studies have been undertaken primarily by the psychologists, although sometimes, anthropologists are active participants in these studies. We shall discuss some of these outstanding experiments and their outcomes. It may be noted here that many experiments on birds and bees, dolphins, horses and dogs although provide evidences that while other animals respond to stimuli-bound messages, the creative linguistic ability is only possessed by the humans, and it would be interesting to note the degree of creativity shared by the anthropoids with man.

In the 1930s, one of the most famous experiments was conducted by psychologists, Winthrop Kellog and Luella Kellog, who raised their infant son together with an infant chimpanzee named Gua. The boy and the chimpanzee were administered with a parallel series of intelligence tests to notice the language ability. It was found that Gua could understand about 100 words at 16 months, and it was more words than the boy could understand. But the chimpanzee could not go beyond that in comprehending the language.

In a similar way, Keith Hayes and Cathy Hayes raised a chimpanzee at home, Viki, who could learn and pronounce a number of individual words . She could even articulate three words, "mama", "papa", and "cup" at appropriate situations. But that was the extent of language production by Viki.

In another experiment, Allen Gardner and Beatrice Gardner trained Washoe, a caught-in-the-wild infant chimpanzee, in sign language, as they thought that the apes were capable of natural use of gestures and manipulation. By the age of 5 years and at the end of the experiment, Washoe could understand and produce more than 100 signs. But it was impossible for Washoe to pick up the grammar of the language.

In another remarkable experiment, David Premack, a psychologist at the University of California, Santa Barbara, tried to teach language to another infant chimpanzee, Sarah. But this time, the language training consisted of differently shaped and coloured plastic symbols with metal backs. The chimp was taught by arranging the symbols on a magnetic board. The chimp was able to respond to many of the questions of the trainer by arranging the symbols on the magnetic board. And it was told that Sarah had even mastered some rules of syntax. This is regarded as one of the most successful experiments on chimpanzee language acquisition. But Sarah did not speak spontaneously, as a human child does in most natural conditions. Another psychologist at the Yerkes primate centre in Georgia has conducted a similar experiment with Lana, a two and half years old chimpanzee, training the chimp with a computer programmed conversation with some success.

Another chimpanzee learning experiment was undertaken under the direction of the psychologist, Herbert Terrace and his associates at Columbia University. The project involved the chimpanzee. Nim Chimpsky and about 100 staff members. In one of the most systematic and well-documented projects till now, Nim was taught by more than 60 teachers, and could learn to express 125 signs during the first forty-four months of training. In a review of the overall performance of Nim, Terrace summarized, "...it would be premature to conclude that a chimpanzee's combinations show the same structure evident in the sentences of a child" (quoted in Akmajian *et al.*, 1984: 489). Even the experiments with the young gorilla, Hanabi-Ko (or Koko) and others could not lead to any convincing answer that the apes did have the capability to speak.

Despite remarkable success of some of these experiments, it is evident from the conclusions drawn so far that imitation is not a substitute for creativity in language. Even some of the talking birds imitate exactly the human sounds, which does not mean that birds can speak. The capacity of producing communicative language among the non-human species is limited to a stimulus-bound response, rather than a spontaneous creative language like the human child speaks. Human linguistic capacity seems to be unparallel in the whole of animal kingdom, as the human ".... children master what appears to be one of the most complex intellectual skills with virtually no formal tuition. From the cacophony of sounds that the infant hears it is able to construct the elements of its native language, so that by age of five it uses perhaps two thousand words of spoken vocabulary and comprehends at least four thousand. . . ." (Leaky, 1982: 184).

ACQUISITION OF LANGUAGE

We know that the human child speaks his language without any flaw before he is 5 years old. The significant aspect of child language acquisition is that nobody consciously teaches the intricacies of grammar and meaning associated with every single word in a language. We have also noted that many experiments with non-human primates have proved to be failures, despite a constant and deliberate teaching of the animal. Therefore, the ability to acquire the language by a human child and using it at his will is the uniqueness of man as the only speaking animal in the world. Although the complexity of the process of acquisition of language by the human child is not completely and authentically understood, psychological and neurological advancements have been helpful in understanding this process to some degree. It is however certain that the human child is equipped with the necessary neural requirements for production and use of language right from its birth.

Our general observation of the nature of human language reveals that the number of words at the disposal of a human child is very limited. Even then, the child is capable of constructing an infinite number of sentences by the processes of permutation and combination of the limited repository of words. In fact, he constructs sentences, most of which he has never produced before. He is also capable of making sense out of many sentences, which he has never heard before. This means that the child learns the rules of grammar of his language effortlessly, which nobody teaches him. It may be remembered that to learn the grammar of a language other than our own, we take most part of our life-time and perhaps end up with less degree of success, which the child masters within hardly 5 years. Not only the rules of complex grammar, but the child also learns easily the social use of language, differentiating between a normal and a taboo word, a polite and impolite construction etc. In other words, by the age of 5, the child masters the communicative competence absolutely naturally.

For a long time, philosophers and behavioural scientists have been trying to find out the secret of this innate capability of the human mind. One of the earliest philosophers and influential figures of liberal Western thought, John Locke (1632—1704) thought that the human mind was an "empty cabinet" and his culture is shaped by the influence of the cultural milieu around him. Locke's theory has been carried forward by the psychologists, J. B. Watson and B. F. Skinner, who proposed that words, their meanings and uses were 'conditioned responses' and were acquired through the process of conditioning by the local linguistic environment. Because of its total applicability in cases of human creativity of languages, modern linguists have been strongly influenced by an alternative theory of language and mind. Before Locke, it was the French philosopher, Rene Descartes (1596—1650), who advocated that knowledge and perception were based on innate ideas or structures of mind, which shape the interpretation of experiences. The application of the this logic to language would mean that some primeval form of language exists in the human mind right at the time of birth, which has a basic pattern common to all men. During the middle of this century, the famous linguist, Noam Chomsky, adopted this view in his study of syntax and emphasized the existence of a uniquely human mental organisation, an innate *deep structure*, which was transformed, in speech, into specific *surface structures*. While the debate continues, we are sure that the human child has an enormous potentiality to acquire language, which follows almost definite successive steps for the children speaking any language in any part of the world.

Stages in Language Acquisition

Immediately after birth, the human child starts crying and in happier moments makes some unrecognisable sounds. Linguists and behavioural scientists do not consider these sounds under the process of acquisition. Because, such sounds are mostly stimulus-controlled and are the involuntary responses to hunger or discomfort. Since these sounds are not creative in the sense of not being free from either external or internal stimuli, these are not considered as the stages of language acquisition. However, the following stages are more or less observed among the children in general, and are nearly universal.

The earliest stage of child's language acquisition is known as the stage of **babbling**. When the child is between 5 and 6 months of age, (s)he babbles or utters some sounds and sound sequences, which are different from the stimulus-controlled cries and gurgles. These sounds are to a large extent meaningless. Even deaf children babble around this age like normal children. While some scholars think that babbling is a necessary prerequisite for later development of the language, some others think it as unimportant. However, as both normal and deaf children pass through the stage of babbling, it is presumed that the human child is biologically predisposed to babble.

When the child is around one year old, he enters into the second stage of language acquisition, which is known as the **holophrastic** or one-word stage. In this stage, the child expresses himself with the help of some one-word 'sentences', which are limited in number. He picks up names for familiar people, animals and objects, which he recognises around him and utters *mama, papa, ball, cup, dog* etc.. Sometimes, he utters some words indicating actions or demands like, *no, not, more* etc. The holophrastic stage of acquisition is particularly characterised by a peculiar phenomenon, commonly referred to as overextension or generalisation of reference. This means that more often the child refers to all animals as *dog,* with which he is more familiar. It is also not surprising that at this age he addresses to all men he encounters as *papa* or all women as *mama.*

When the child is around 2 years old, he begins to produce **two-word** utterances, although some children attain this stage slightly earlier or later. The utterances at this stage are marked by the absence of syntactic or morphological markers and the use of pronouns are extremely rare. Usually, during this stage, the child speaks simple noun+noun words like, *mama shoe, hi papa, cat bad, baby chair* etc., which are devoid of any marker for number or person or tense. By this age, the child articulates about 50 different words and becomes an entertaining partner in conversation.

In the next stage of acquisition, the child utters two, three, four, five or more words together and comparisons between the children are usually made by the *mean length of utterances* or MLU rather than by chronological age. The most significant feature of this stage is that the child expresses the words mostly in a telegraphic manner and hence, these utterances are also known as **telegraphic speech**. Some of the common occurrences during this stage are : *what that?, he play little tune, mummy come, no sit there, cat drink milk* and so on. This however exemplifies the capability of the child to grasp the principles of sentence formation. Gradually, the child with the growing age, picks up the syntactic or the grammatical rules of the language and acquires to use the inflectional and derivational morphemes. By the age of 3 years, the child articulates about 100 different words easily and his pronunciation becomes closer to the adult language. By the time the child is about 4 years old, he is fully capable of acquiring the adult language and becomes a part of his linguistic community.

In order to explain as to how the child manages to acquire the adult language, various theories have been proposed. One of these theories, the **imitation theory**, proposes that as the human child constantly imitates the language of the adults around him, gradually he also picks up the intricacies of the syntax and sentence construction. But this theory seems to be untenable, as the child commits the mistakes repeatedly, despite his hearing the adult speech in its corrected version all the time. There is yet another theory, known as the **reinforcement theory,** which suggests that the constant positive reinforcement for the correct utterances and negative reinforcement for the wrong utterances prompt the child to correct himselfand then, gradually picks up the adult speech. But this is operationally found to be untrue, as the mistakes committed by the children at this age are regraded as 'cute' and enjoyed rather than the child is reprimanded. However, both imitation and reinforcement theories fail as these views do not account for the fact that children are capable of constructing their own rules for the purpose of sentence construction. The available knowledge at the moment is not sufficient enough to convincingly answer the details of this innate device of language acquisition by the human child, which is characteristically different from other animals.

Second Language Acquisition

It is a fairly well-known fact that when a child grows up in a multilingual environment, he starts speaking a second language other than his mother-tongue quite easily. But an adult person sometimes takes his whole life time to speak a second language. Perhaps, the difficulty lies in the distinction between the processes of **acquisition** and **learning**. While acquisition is a process of gradual development of using a language in communicative situations, learning is a very conscious process of mastering the vocabulary and grammar of a language. Therefore, an adult person **learns** a second language rather than **acquires,** which most certainly a child does. Experiences also show that even in an ideal acquisition situation, an adult can very rarely acquire native-like proficiency in using a second language. It is believed that after the critical period of acquisition, which is around the time of puberty, it becomes difficult to master another language because the language-faculty by this time is already set and its flexibility is lost to a greater extent. Some other opinions are that the 'optimum age' of language acquisition is between 11 and 16 years of age and not the early teens. However, in order to learn a second language some methods have been devised and we shall discuss some of them.

The most traditional method to learn a second language is the **grammar-translation** method. In this method, an emphasis is placed on the written rather than the spoken language. The learner has to memorise a long list of words and a set of grammatical rules. This however does not equip the learner to master the intricacies of the use of the vocabulary in linguistically appropriate contexts.

As a contrast to the grammar-translation method, there is another approach, which puts emphasis on the spoken language and not on the written language. This method is commonly known as the **direct** method. In the class room everything is expressed in the second language, so that the learner thinks and expresses in that language and picks it up in passing. This method is also told not to be very effective for many children.

In order to make the learning process a bit more rigorous, another method called the **audio-lingual** method is suggested. It emphasises more on structured material for the student, starting from simpler and moving on to more complex grammatical constructions and repeated drilling or practice of learning. Although it appears monotonous and boring, this helps the child in picking up the language mechanically.

A relatively recent method of acquiring the second language is described as the **communicative** method. This method emphasises the learning of the function of the language rather than its form. The lessons in this method are organised around activities in various social contexts and not by giving a high degree of grammatical input.

Whatever method may be adopted for the acquisition of the second language, if the age of the learner is above the optimum, the influence or interference of the first language is very conspicuously noticed while speaking the second language with native accent. The best example could be a Korean or a Japanese, or an Indian speaking English in his own characteristic way.

DEVELOPMENT OF WRITING

According to a Chinese proverb, "the palest ink is better than the sharpest memory" (quoted in Fromkin and Rodman, 1978: 356). The truth of the proverb is being felt today. In the previous section we outlined that Australopithecus could probably speak some kind of language about 2 million years ago. But we are not certain due to the lack of any kind of definite evidence about this proposition. Therefore, all our reconstructions are finally speculative. Had Australopithecus written something about his language somewhere, the speculation could have been turned into facts. But there is an inherent problem in this. By his genetic constitution, man is a talking animal, or talking is an innate attribute of man and not writing. That is why, there are millions of people in today's world who speak every moment but are unable to write. Therefore, it is certain that after thousands of years of speaking, man first started writing. Although we are again not sure when man started writing first, on the basis of some earliest available evidences, we are trying to reconstruct the stages of writing.

It is widely believed that the earliest form of writing are the **cave drawings** that we see in various parts of the world. In India, we have many cave paintings in Bhimbhetka in Madhya Pradesh and other places, which are dated back to the upper palaeolithic period of the human prehistory. Excellent cave drawings have also been found from Altamira in north Spain depicting the aspects of the life of the contemporary man giving us an indication of earliest human writings. It is believed that all these drawings are about 20,000 years old. From the upper palaeolithic remains, we also get some engravings on bone tools, which testify the earliest forms of writing.

The next stage of development of writing was possibly represented by **pictograms** or writing through pictures. Unlike modern writing systems, each picture or pictogram is a direct image of the object it represents. In other words, in this form of writing, there is a non-arbitrary relationship between the form and meaning of the picture and it shows a high degree of consistency. Hence, it does not represent any language as such, except the object of reference. Interestingly, although it is believed that ancient man was using pictograms to speak about objects, these are very much in use today throughout the world, irrespective of the literary achievements. It is used among African tribes, American Indians, Alaskan Eskimos, streets of New York or London as signs of parking places, public toilets, restricted areas, railway and bus stations, theatres and so on. The advantage of the pictographic writing is that it can be understood by anyone from any linguistic background.

The next stage of development of writing was probably in the form of **ideograms**. Ideogram literally means the idea pictures or idea writing. In this form, the picture represents not exactly the object itself, but its attributes. For example, the picture of a sun could also represent warmth, heat, light, day, brilliance and so on. These are the ideas associated with sun and a picture of sun could mean anything from this list. In course of time, pictograms and ideograms became stylised and hence, it became difficult to interpret the meaning from the pictorial presentations. This period also marked the transformation of the pictograms into linguistic symbols with arbitrary relationship between the form and meaning of the pictures. In Egyptian hieroglyphics, for example, 𓉐 was used to refer to a house and in Chinese writing, 川 is used for a river, which are symbolic abstractions from the real world objects themselves. When the relationship between the symbol and the idea became sufficiently abstract, symbols represented words in a language, which came to be known as **logograms**, as we see the derived symbol ~~~ for water in Egyptian writing.

The ancient Sumerians, who built a civilisation in southern Mesopotamia. the south of modern Iraq, over 5000 years ago present to us the earliest form of writing. It is believed that the Sumerians were flourishing traders and they had the necessity of permanent record keeping, which prompted the development of writing among them.

The Sumerian pictograms evolved into what is known as **cuneiform** writing by using a wedge-shaped stylus, where the symbol represented the name of the thing than the actual thing itself.

The inscriptions used by the Sumerians were produced by pressing a wedge-shaped implement into soft clay tablets, resulting in 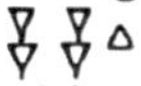 forms. It is now believed that the Sumerians had a true word writing system. Attempts have also been made to decipher the meaning of symbols used by the people of the Indus Valley civilisation about 3500 years ago and further research in this direction might throw some light into the ancient writing system in the Indian sub-continent.

Gradually, a single sign was increasingly used to represent all words with the same sound or the homophones of the language. This principle was named as **rebus** and culminated in the rebus writing system. For example, the sign of an eye could represent the pronoun 'I' or the sign of the sun could similarly represent 'son'. The word, belief, was represented by the sign of a 'bee' and the sign of a 'leaf'. Although not in itself a very efficient system, the rebus writing led to a syllabic writing system with many advantages over the rebus system.

The ancient Babylonians and Persians adopted the cuneiform of writing from the ancient Sumerians and used them to represent the sounds of the syllables in their words. Thus, the cuneiform evolved into the system of **syllabic writing**. In a syllabic writing system, each syllable in the language is represented by its own symbol. Words are written by juxtaposing the symbols of their individual syllables. By around 500 B.C., the Persians had devised a simplified syllabic alphabet for their language.

Around 4000 B.C., when the Sumerian pictography was at its peak, a similar system was in vogue in Egypt, which is known as **hieroglyphics**, literally meaning sacred carvings. The hieroglyphs represented the sounds of the words they symbolised. Slowly it emerged as a word writing system and was borrowed by many people in its advanced syllabic stage. In course of time, the Greeks invented the modern **alphabetic** writing system. In fact, the word alphabet is derived from the first two letters of the Greek alphabet, *alpha* and *beta*. The alphabetic system became the system of writing, where each symbol represented one phoneme or the sound unit. Scholars believe that the Greek alphabetic writing system was passed on to the Italians, who passed it in turn to the Romans. Later, the Christian missionaries used alphabetic system for translating the Holy Bible into many languages for the benefit of millions of preliterate people in the world. Another line of development took the Greek writing system into East Europe, where slavic languages were spoken. The modification there came to be known as **cyrillic** alphabet, which is the basis of modern Russian system of writing.

3

HISTORY OF LINGUISTIC THOUGHT

LINGUISTICS IN THE 19TH CENTURY AND BEFORE

In 1957, a revolution occurred in the field of linguistics with the appearance of the theory of transformational-generative grammar by Noam Chomsky, who is undoubtedly one of the most innovative thinkers of our time. Chomsky himself stresses the relationship of his own work with that of the 18th century German linguist, Wilhelm von Humboldt (1767-1835) and of the rationalist philosophers of the 17th century France. Therefore, although most of the theoretical developments in linguistics took place at the beginning of the 20th century, like other branches of knowledge, it is mostly a cumulative effort, and is integrated with the linguistic thinking of the past.

Ancient India, as in many other fields of knowledge, had excelled in the field of language research. India's first great grammarian, **Panini**, is regarded even today as the father of Sanskrit grammar. Panini had written his principles of grammar with the help of 4000 *sutras* or aphorisms, composed with the symbolic brevity of the most concise *memoria technica*. But Panini himself had acknowledged at least ten great Indian grammarians before him, and one of them was Yaska, whose writings date back to the middle of the 4th century B.C. After Panini, however, the tradition of linguistic research in India was further reinforced with **Katyayana's** *Varttika* or supplementary rules of grammar, **Patanjali's** *Maha Bhashya* or commentary on Panini, and **Kaiyata's** comments on Patanjali and so on. Therefore, the history of linguistics in India goes back approximately to the middle of the 4th century B.C., according to the most moderate estimate. In the West, linguistics was mostly the interest of philosophers before the

19th century. It is significant that the Greek philosophers made a very substantial contribution to the science of linguistics, and it is said that Plato was the first to distinguish between nouns and verbs.

Some people believe that the birth date of modern linguistics is 1786, as the first foundation of comparative linguistics was laid down during this year. On 2 February 1786, a British Judge in colonial India and an ardent student of linguistics, **Sir William Jones**, said in a speech delivered at the Asiatic Society, Calcutta: "The *Sanscrit* language... is of a wonderful structure; more perfect than the *Greek*, more copious than the *Latin*, and more exquisitely refined than either, yet bearing to both of them a stronger affinity, both in the roots of verbs and in the forms of grammar, than could possibly have been produced by accident; . . . no philologer could examine them all three, without believing them to have sprung from some common source, which, perhaps, no longer exists: there is a similar reason. . . . for supposing that both the *Gothick* and the *Celtick*... had the same origin with the *Sanscrit;* and the old *Persian* might be added to the same family" (quoted in Simpson, 1981: 20, italics in original). Jones' remarks highlighted for the first time that the great Indian language, Sanskrit, and other European languages like, Greek, Latin, Celtic and Germanic had striking structural similarities. Because of these similarities, Jones believed that all these languages might have originated from a common source. This idea excited many, like Friedrich von Schlegel and others, and there were many serious attempts to prove this, culminating in a hypothetical ancestor of all these languages, the Proto-Indo-European. After this, the general intellectual atmosphere for quite some time remained preoccupied with the pursuit of this exercise, which is commonly referred to as 'classical philology'.

The change of emphasis from classical philology to modern linguistics occurred originally in Germany. The conventional study of Indo-European languages went hand in hand with the intellectual and artistic movement from the late-18th to mid-19th century in Germany, known as Romanticism. It was a movement which rejected the classical tradition and emphasised indigenous, ethnic and cultural roots. "Since race, language and culture were assumed to be intimately related, reconstruction of the prehistory of the

Germanic and other language-stock was attractive to the Romantic temperament" (Sampson, 1980: 14).

TABLE 3.1 : **Indo-European Sound Correspondences**

Indo-European	*Sanskrit*	*Latin*	*English*
p	pitar-	pater	father
t	trayas	tres	three
k	—	canis	hound
b	—	labium	lip
d	dva	duo	two
g	—	ager	acre
bh	bhratar-	frater	brother
dh	dha	fe-ci	do
gh	vah-	veh-o	wagon

During the 19th century, while the influence of German Romanticism on the study of linguistics continued, it was also greatly influenced by the general state of science at that time. Sampson notes that during this period, there were two outstandingly successful scientific paradigms, the salient features of which were also reflected in the history-centered outlook of the 19th century linguists. The first of these paradigms was mechanistic physics, which stated that "all phenomena could be described by simple, deterministic laws of force and motion—so that all future states of the world could in principle be inferred from a complete knowledge of its present state. . .". The philologists followed this paradigm and some of them looked for the universal 'laws' of sound change in a language. The most successful of these was Grimm's Law, which accounted for phonological changes in the Germanic languages. **Jakob Grimm** had shown in 1822 that in Germanic languages, bh, dh, gh, b, d, g, p, t, and k, sounds were changed into b, d, g, p, t, k, f, th, and x (or h) respectively, which did not happen in the case of Sanskrit, Greek or Latin. In fact, the fundamental principles underlying these comparisons were first laid down in 1814 by Rasmus Rask (1787-1832), not published till 1818.

The second source of inspiration for contemporary linguistics, other than mechanistic physics, was the outstanding developments in the field of biological sciences. Eventually, many linguists of the time regarded language as a natural phenomenon on par with plants and animals. Even before the publication of Darwin's *Origin of Species,* August Pott wrote in 1833, "A language is in a constant state of change throughout its life: like every organic object (*organische Naturgegenstand*), it has its period of gestation and maturation, times of accelerated and of slackened growth, its prime, decay and gradual extinction. . . ." (quoted in *ibid* : 17). But with the publication of Darwin's *Origin of Species*, there were attempts to chart the evolution of language alongside the evolution of organic species. In 1863, an influential linguist of the contemporary times, August Schleicher published a short treatise on *Darwin's Theory and Linguistics*, drawing a theoretical parallel between linguistics and the natural sciences. In fact, the linguists regarded the language-families, languages, dialects and idiolects, as corresponding to what biologists would name phyla, orders, genera, species and individuals. They also believed that languages and language-families constantly compete with one another, exactly like the species fight among themselves in a 'struggle for survival'. Schleicher even went to the extent of arguing that the theory of evolution could be better confirmed in language than with respect to the plant and animal kingdoms. Therefore, till the end of the 19th century, it was presumed that the historical approach was the natural one for the study of language; it was the era of **historical linguistics** with a strong biological influence. But towards the end of the century, the biological analogy came under severe criticism. Initially, the linguists accepted that the direction of language change exactly follows the direction of biological change, that is, from simpler forms to more complex forms. As unicellular organisms transform into highly complex organisms in the course of evolution, so languages pass through three phases in order of their complexity : *isolating, agglutinating* and *inflecting*. In isolating languages, each word has a single unchanging root, while in agglutinating languages words include affixes as well as roots; and in inflecting languages, one word denotes many different meaning units. Other linguists divided languages into *synthetic* and *analytic* and proposed that languages changed from synthetic (or inflecting) to analytic (incorporating the characters of isolating type), directly contradicting the evolutionary paradigm of isolating—

agglutinating—inflecting type. This and other controversies during this period led to the reconsideration of the nature of human language. The biological analogy of the causes and directions of language change and the theory of the survival of the fittest seemed to be more and more unconvincing to scholars towards the end of the 19th century, and it no longer appeared to offer a more prestigious paradigm as it did towards the middle of the century. Since historical linguistics remained no more fascinating and was constantly under controversy, the beginning of the next century was perhaps the best time to think of an alternative to the conventional theory of historical linguistics.

DE SAUSSURE AND STRUCTURAL STUDY OF LANGUAGE

When the organic analogy utterly failed in explaining the nature of a non-tangible 'object" like a language, there arose an acute need to devise a suitable method to understand it. At this juncture, the Swiss linguist, Mongin-Ferdinand de Saussure (1857-1913) proposed a revolutionary method to understand language, which was different from the conventional historical or comparative approaches, just aiming at finding out the origin and relationship between different languages. He epitomised the shift in emphasis from comparative or historical linguistics to descriptive or synchronic linguistics, and hence, is regarded as the father of modern 20th century linguistics.

Saussure was born in Geneva in 1857 into a scholarly family. He was trained in conventional historical linguistics and was very successful in it at a very early age. He had shown merit in his early publications on the reconstruction of the Proto-Indo-European languages. Later, he started teaching philology at the *Ecole Pratique des Hautes Etudes* in Paris, from 1881 to 1891, before he returned to Geneva to a chair in linguistics. At the request of a colleague, Saussure took over a course on general linguistics at the end of 1906 and continued teaching it in 1908-1909 and again in 1910-1911. During the initial years, Saussure mostly talked about conventional historical linguistics and only towards the end, in his introduction to the course, he included some of his outstanding ideas on structural linguistics. Not long after that, in 1913, Saussure died, but two of his colleagues, Charles Bally and Albert Sachehaye, who were greatly excited by his ideas, but could not hear him because of their own teaching commitments, collected the class notes from Saussure's students, collected the remains of his lecture notes, and in 1916, published the revolutionary book entitled, *Cours de linguistique generale*. With this posthumous publication, Saussure became a celebrity in the field of linguistics.

The major point of difference between the conventional varieties of historical linguistics and Saussure's view was the way the language ought to be treated. Saussure felt that in the piecemeal analysis of language, like the change of a particular morpheme into another, one does not speak anything about the language *per se*. Therefore, he proposed, language should be studied as a **system**, where each part was intimately related to all other parts, and any change in any one of the parts essentially brought about tremendous change in the whole of the language. In other words, each small part of a language is just redundant in itself and only acquires meaning in relation to others. In his book, *Cours*, he draws an analogy between language and the game of chess. He says, "....if I use ivory chessmen instead of wooden ones, the change has no effect on the system, but if I increase or decrease the number of chessmen, this change has a profound effect on the 'grammar' of the game". This implies that the chessboard remains at any given time in a state of equilibrium, where each item acquires value in relation to the other and any slight change or move has a far-reaching effect on the game. He says, "A certain move can revolutionise the whole game and even affect pieces that are not immediately involved". He assigns an exactly similar character to language by saying that at any given point of time, language maintains a kind of equilibrium or a 'language state' (*etat de langue*) and, therefore, language can be viewed as an intact system at any time, without regard to its history. This was the aspect of the language which was not stressed before, and nobody till that time had seriously examined the relationship between one item and the rest in a language. His insistence that language was a system of interwoven structures led to the emergence of a new field of study, namely **structural linguistics.**

Behind Saussure's suppositions of the 'systemic' nature of language and its maintenance of a 'language state' or *etat de langue*, was a subtle yet very important distinction between the **synchronic** and **diachronic** approaches to the study of language. For him, whatever other virtues historical linguistics might have, it told nothing about how the language functions from the 'point of view of those who use it', since for the speaker of a language, its history does not exist (Sampson *op cit.* : 36). If one attempts to describe a language from the outside (an etic perspective), from the position of an 'observer' rather than of a 'participant', one can take either the synchronic or the diachronic approach. But to describe the language as an insider (an emic perspective), one has to look at it synchronically, because for an insider, language has no time extension, except its present form of systemic structure. This relationship between synchrony and the systemic language state can again be explained with the help of an example from the chess board. The black queen at a centre position may be very advantageous to Black and not to the White, and hence, the value of any piece depends on all others at that particular point of time in the game. The same logic is applicable to language as well. Saussure's example in this context is the English word *sheep*. Conventionally, English *sheep* is the equivalent of French *mutton*. But in English, *sheep* contrasts with *mutton* unlike in French. This makes Saussure's point very clear that every word in a language is meaningful with respect to that language at that point of time, which may not be true for other languages or for the same language at different points of time. Therefore, in Saussure's formulations, the synchronic approach is exemplified as *the* approach to study the structure of language.

In the *Cours*, Saussure next addresses the question as to what language is ? He suggests that languages are 'social facts', without of course using the exact terminology. Here we find the sharing of ideas between the French sociologist, Emile Durkheim and Saussure, both of whom were contemporaries. Durkheim proposed the notion of 'social fact' in his *Rules of Sociological Method* (1895), which represented the ideas in the collective mind. "The collective mind of a society is something that exists over and above the individual members of the society, and its ideas are only indirectly and imperfectly reflected in the minds of the people who make up that society" (*ibid.* : 44). We are aware that every social system devises some general rules or codes of conduct, which anthropologists sometimes call 'norms', and the behaviour of a normal individual is guided and regulated by these norms, which he shares as a member of that particular society. Therefore, for Durkheim, social facts have concrete effects, and these are 'things' as real as stones or other physical objects, but belonging to a different logical category. In a similar fashion, Saussure conceived that language fitted into the category of social facts. But he insisted that one should draw a distinction between the physical facts that could be tangibly observed (the actual speaking), which he called ***parole***, and the general intangible system of language or ***langue***, which lies at the level of the collective mind. Hence, Saussure says that while *parole* (speech) is produced by individual speakers, ". . . language is not complete in any speaker; it exists perfectly only within a collectivity".

Saussure believed that a language comprised of a set of signs. Each sign, in turn, was the union of a ***signifiant*** or a 'signifier' represented by a portion of speech sound, and a ***signifie*** or a 'signified' representing a portion of meaning. He said that no individual sign could be considered in isolation, because both their pronunciation and meaning were governed by their contrasts with other signs of the language system. In other words, the language provides us with a system, which is the basis for individuating sounds or concepts, and without which the sound is meaningless. A close parallel to this could be drawn from the anthropological examples of kinship terminology. Each kin term is understood with the help of a social and cultural system, without which it acquires no meaning. The distinction between MB (Mother's Brother) in south and north Indian kinship systems could be taken as a case in point. While in the south Indian system MB (*mama*) means potential father-in-law, thus putting the term under the classificatory kin term category, in the north Indian system, it remains as a descriptive one.

Saussure's proposition of the systemic nature of language has another obvious culmination in the form of more emphasis on the 'contrasts' in the language. This led to the distinction between **syntagmatic**, and **associative** or **paradigmatic** relations in a language. While syntagmatic relations are the ways that linguistic units can be combined into longer constructions and based upon linearity, paradigmatic relations are those between elements that can substitute for one another in the same place in a linguistic structure. The following example will help us in understanding the differences between the two:

The village was flooded.
The farmhouse was flooded.

Here we can observe that the words, *village* and *farmhouse* are related to each other in a mutually substitutable way, and the substitution does not in any way affect the **form** of the sentence, except changing its **content**. Therefore, these words are paradigmatically related to one another as contrast sets. But in the same sentences, the words, *the, village, was* and *flooded* constitute linguistic units that are combined into longer constructions. The substitution of any one of these words with any other, brings about change in the form of the sentence. Saussure's argument was that the value of a linguistic element depended on the elements with which it contrasted and hence, he was more interested in paradigmatic relations between the linguistic units than the syntagmatic relation between them. Because of this legacy, European linguistics has been more interested in the study of paradigmatic relations rather than syntagmatic relations, the latter being more often associated with American linguistics. Saussure's view of language as a social fact and his distinction between *langue* and *parole* were accepted without much disagreement for about four decades till the publications of Noam Chomsky appeared in the late 1950s, making Saussure's ideas again a live issue.

THE PRAGUE SCHOOL OF FUNCTIONAL LINGUISTICS

While Saussure was lecturing on his innovative ideas of structural linguistics in 1911 in Geneva, two other similar yet independent developments opposed to the method of traditional philology were taking place. The first came from Franz Boas in the U.S.A. with the publication of *Handbook of American Indian Languages, Part I* (1911), published by the Smithsonian Institution, which we shall discuss in subsequent sections of this chapter. The second came from a Czech Anglicist, Vilem Mathesius (1882-1945), who studied and subsequently taught at the Caroline University of Prague. In February, 1911, he delivered a trend-setting lecture in Prague, *On the Potentiality of the Phenomena of Language*. When some like-minded scholars joined Mathesius and met for regular discussions from 1926 onwards till the outbreak of the Second World War, it came to be recognised as the 'Prague School' of linguistics.

Prague linguistics, in general, saw language in terms of function, or more specifically, was inclined to show the respective functions played by various structural components in the use of the entire language. Sampson is of the opinion that Prague linguistics ". . . looked at language as one might look at a motor, seeking to understand what jobs the various components were doing and how the nature of one component determined the nature of others. As long as they were describing the structure of language, the practice of the Prague School was not very different from that of their contemporaries. . .but they tried to go beyond description to explanation, saying not just *what* languages were like but *why* they were the way they were" (Sampson, *op cit.*: 104). Although Mathesius is regarded as the founder of the movement, it was Prince Nikolai Sergeyevich Trubetzkoy (1890-1938), who was responsible for giving direction to the movement and Professor Roman Jakobson (1896-1982), who had extended the Prague School theory and practice into new areas. Although there have been many refinements and modifications in the techniques of linguistic analysis since the time of Mathesius and Trubetzkoy, let us very briefly examine some of the contributions of the founders of the School.

Trubetzkoy was born into a scholarly family of Russian nobles. He was a student of Indo-European linguistics at the University of Moscow and later became a member of staff there in 1916. Because of political reasons, he had to leave Moscow, and after a few detours, reached Vienna, where he was appointed to the chair of Slavonic philology in 1922. He remained in Vienna till his death in 1938 and struggled to finish his book, *Principles of Phonology*, in the last weeks of his life. During his stay in Vienna, he was associated with Prague School, although he was staying about 150 miles away from Prague. Trubetzkoy and his associates contemplated on the study of phonology, which they defined as the study of the function of speech-sounds, justifying their functionalist stand. Basic to their method of sound structuring is the use of contrast or opposition, for they believed that it was possible to construct a system of interrelationships only by establishing the differences between the phonemes. Here, we are reminded of the stress on paradigmatic rather than syntagmatic relationships proposed by Saussure, which was reinforced in the tradition of the Prague linguistics. For Trubetzkoy, a phoneme is a bundle of simultaneous distinctive features consisting of binary contrasts and oppositions, being simply the sum of these binary contrasts, and having validity only in a given *and relative* set of phonetic contrasts (Waterman, 1963: 72). Lévi-Strauss, however, summarises the stand taken by Trubetzkoy with regard to phonological method, which eventually inspired him to propose structural method in anthropology. He says, "...he (Trubetzkoy) reduces in brief, the phonological method to four fundamental steps: in the first place, phonology passes from the study of *conscious* linguistics phenomena to that of their underlying *unconscious* structure; it refuses to take *terms* as independent entities, on the contrary it takes *relations* between terms as the basis of its analysis; it introduces the notion of *system*. . . .; finally, it aims at the discovery of *general laws* either found by induction 'or. . .deduced logically, which gives them an absolute character' (1933, p. 243)" (Lévi-Strauss, in Hymes, 1964: 41).

Roman Osipovich Jakobson is another scholar of Russian origin and was trained in Oriental languages at the University of Moscow. He studied and taught at Prague and Brno till he was forced to leave for the U.S.A. for political exile. In 1949, Jakobson moved to Harvard and from 1957 was associated with the MIT, which became the focus of the modern revolution in linguistics. But during his early years, he became one of the guiding forces of the Prague School and his later writings reflect the intellectual interest of the Prague School as a whole. Although he wrote a great deal on the structuralist approach to literature, his profound influence on the discipline of linguistics is by way of his phonological theory. "The essence of Jakobson's approach to phonology is the notion that there is a relatively simple, orderly universal 'psychological system' of sounds underlying the chaotic wealth of different kinds of sound observed by the phonetician" (Sampson, *op cit.*: 118).

Although the general intellectual orientation of the Prague scholars was to a large extent influenced by the structural linguistics of Saussure, they differed from Saussure with respect to his distinction between synchronic and diachronic approaches to the study of language. It may be recalled that Saussure's *langue* was not applicable to historical investigations and his socially oriented approach minimised the importance and significance of the historical study of language. But in 1928, for the first time, Trubetzkoy, Jakobson and Karcevskij presented a manifesto to the First International Congress of Linguistics at The Hague, where they maintained that phonological methods are equally applicable to diachronic as well as synchronic studies. Since then. Prague linguistics has made distinctive contributions in the area of diachronic linguistics, which was further carried forward by scholars such as Andre Martinet.

STRUCTURAL ANALYSIS IN LINGUISTICS AND ANTHROPOLOGY

Developments in linguistics have very often influenced anthropology more than any other branch of the social sciences. In a seminal article entitled, "Structural Analysis in Linguistics and in Anthropology", **Lévi-Strauss** (1908 -) has attempted to analyse in anthropological data with the help of linguistic models, particularly, after concrete researches on phonology. The relationship between anthropology and linguistics, however, is very old and intimate. Lévi-Strauss says that while the linguist provides etymologies to the anthropologist to permit establishing relations between kinship terms, the anthropologist informs the linguist of customs, prescriptions and prohibitions etc. in a culture to explain the persistence or instability of terms or groups of terms in a linguistic community. But he also believes that till 1920, when Mauss began to write that "Sociology would certainly be much more advanced if it had proceeded everywhere by imitating linguists. . .", the founders of modern linguistics like de Saussure and Antoine Meillet were deliberately under the patronage of the sociologists.

However, Lévi-Strauss believes that the birth of phonology was not only a turning point in linguistics, but rather "...a transformation of this scope is not confined to a particular discipline".

Lévi-Strauss begins with the innovations in phonology as suggested by Trubetzkoy. It may be recollected that Trubetzkoy says that phonology passes from conscious linguistic phenomena to their underlying unconscious structure. Lévi-Strauss draws the analogy by saying that 'kinship systems' like 'phonological systems' are elaborated by the mind at the level of unconscious thought. Secondly, like phonemes, kinship terms are functionally important. Thirdly, both of them acquire this function only after being integrated into their respective systems. And finally, as in phonology, the observable phenomena in kinship result from the play of general, but hidden, laws. This analogy between phonology on the one hand and kinship on the other, led Lévi-Strauss to believe that ". . . . in *another order of reality*, the phenomena of kinship are phenomena of the *same type* as linguistic phenomena". In order to detect the general laws of structure of social systems, Lévi-Strauss again goes back to linguistic methods by insisting that it could be done at the "microsociological" level, as a linguist does by analysing the phonemes into differential elements, which are then organised into one or more pairs of oppositions. For example, he says, the term *father* in our kinship system can be characterised positively with regard to sex (+male; – female), relative age (+ older; – younger), generation (+ ascending; – descending), but negatively with regard to marriage. He however apprehends that by exactly following the phonological principles, finally we end up with a formula like the term "husband" is equal to $C^{2a\ 2d/0}SU^{1}ag/Ego$, and therefore, "...the hypothesis has no explanatory value; it does not make the nature of the system comprehensible; still less does it permit one to reconstruct its origin". He attributes too literal adherence of linguistic methods for the problem of this kind.

In order to discover meaning in kinship nomenclature, he suggests that kinship systems comprise two quite different orders of reality. The first is a system of terminology, through which various kinds of relationships are expressed. The second is a system of attitudes, which are both psychological and social in nature. He disagrees with Radcliffe-Brown that attitudes are nothing but the expression or transposition of terms on the affective level. He takes the example of avanculate relationship to prove that different forms of avanculate can coexist with the same type of descent, whether patrilineal or matrilineal. But four fundamental relationship between four pairs of oppositions (father-son, mother's brother-sister's son, husband-wife, and brother-sister) are required to construct the system. Symbolically, + indicates free and familiar relations, and – stands for hostility, antagonism or reserve. He asserts that to understand the avanculate and a relationship within a system, the structure of which rests upon four terms, i.e. brother, sister, father and son, which are linked by two pairs of oppositions in such a way that in each of the two generations there is one positive and one negative relation. He calls this as *the unit of kinship*. He adds that for the existence of such a kinship structure, three types of family relations must have to be present: a relation of consanguinity, a relation of affinity, and a relation of descent, represented by a relation between siblings, a relation between spouses, and a relation between parent and child. The system of basic attitudes among these relations are comprised of an attitude of mutuality, reciprocity, rights and obligations. Lévi-Strauss however cautions that in many systems, the relationship between two individuals is often expressed not by a single attitude, but by several attitudes which together form a 'bundle', as in case of Trobrianders, where the relationship between husband and wife is characterised by both mutuality and reciprocity. Lévi-Strauss concludes by saying that "A kinship system does not consist in the objective ties of descent or consanguinity between individuals. It exists only in human consciousness; it is an arbitrary system of representations, not the spontaneous development of a real situation". The structural analysis of anthropological phenomena by Lévi-Strauss has attracted both admiration and criticism by many anthropologists. But so far as his kinship analysis is concerned, the British anthropologist, Edmund Leach writes that ". . .Lévi-Strauss here confuses the notion of *descent*, a legal principle governing the transmission of rights from generation to generation, with the notion of *filiation*, the kinship link between parent and child" (Leach, 1974: 101).

AMERICAN DESCRIPTIVISM

In 1911 Franz Boas published his *Handbook of American Indian Languages. Part I*, and set a direction for American linguistics, which was popularly known as descriptivist linguistics. The introduction of this volume is still an excellent introduction to descriptive linguistics. **Franz Boas** (1858-1942) was born in Westphalia and was trained in physics and geography. Later, he became interested in anthropology and was responsible for much of the growth of anthropology in the U.S.A. After a short spell of teaching in Berlin, Boas settled in America in the late 1880s. Under the sponsorship of the Smithsonian Institution, Boas undertook the survey of many indigenous languages of North America and established himself as a great teacher of many second generation linguistic anthropologists. In his introduction to *Handbook of American Indian Languages*, Boas demonstrates the relationship between linguistics and anthropology. He discusses this in terms of two interrelated issues. One is the practical need for an anthropologist to learn the language of the indigenous people where (s)he intends to work, because there are topics like poetry, prayers, oratory and personal and local names, which could be most effectively approached through learning the local language. The second one is more theoretical, as there are a whole lot of 'unconscious phenomena'—such as the classification of ideas and expressed by same or related terms, metaphors and their uses etc. —which can only be best understood by learning the indigenous language. Therefore, even in the theoretical study of the indigenous languages, Boas empirically looked for the cultural root. In his view, "...the description of an individual language was an end in itself, or a necessary first step towards understanding the wider culture of a particular community" (Sampson, *op.cit.*: 59). The abstract linguistic theorising, for him and other descriptivists, was a means to an end of practical description of particular languages, rather than thinking of individual languages as sources of data for the construction of a general theory of language (*ibid.*: 59). It is however true that many of the descriptivists did theorise about language in general, but all their theorisations were based on intensive research on the detailed structure of different indigenous languages. Because of this emphasis on the description of exotic languages, linguistics in America developed in departments and centres of anthropology, and remained as an integral part of it. Although Boas may be regarded as the founder of the school of American descriptivism, it was Leonard Bloomfield who was the most influential figure in American linguistics during the first half of this century, and the principal representative of the school.

Leonard Bloomfield (1887-1949) had studied linguistics in the traditional style and had spent some time in Leipzig and Gottingen in association with the great figures of the contemporary neo-grammarian movement. Before he became the Professor of Linguistics at Yale in 1940, Bloomfield taught Germanic philology at different Universities. He took up the study of American Indian languages of the Algonquian family and some indigenous languages of the Philippines. Although he followed the Boasian tradition of descriptive linguistics, he strived to establish the status of linguistics as a science. As Bernard Bloch rightly observes in the journal, *Language*: "There can be no doubt that Bloomfield's greatest contribution to the study of language was to make a science of it" (XXV, 92). Bloomfield became an active proponent of positivist ideas as they applied to the study of human behaviour, including language. To Bloomfield, the principle of regularity of sound-change was the cornerstone of linguistic science. He championed the neo-grammarian position vigorously and without compromise. He, however, improved upon Grimm and neo-grammarians by restating their findings in physical terms, that is, in the language of the scientific description. He gave up figurative, metaphysical expressions, always searching for the everyday words of the physical world. His book, *Language* (1933) continues to be of greatest influence although linguistics has gone beyond Bloomfield now. While Bloomfield was more interested in the mechanistic statement of all meanings with a relative neglect to the study of semantics, his contemporary, **Edward Sapir** (1884-1939) ranged widely through and around his subject, finding out its relations with literature, music, anthropology, and psychology, thus insisting the influence of language on every department of human life. His *Selected Writings* in Mandelbaum's *Language, Culture and Personality* (1949) shows the width of his scholarship, for which he is still read not only by the linguists, but also by anthropologists and psychologists. Descriptivism in general had a shortcoming in that one of its key principles was that a general theory of human language was unimportant and hence, less of emphasis on theorisation and more on the analytic practice. Therefore, although descriptivism has not died out in America, it has been pushed from the centre of the stage to the wings, and Chomskyan linguistics has taken its place.

Chomsky and the Revolution in Linguistics

As has already been said, Chomsky remains among the most innovative thinkers of our times, a scholar who has given a new direction to linguistics, not only in America, but in the world of linguistics generally. **Avram Noam Chomsky** was born in Philadelphia in 1928 into a family of politically radical Jews of Russian descent. His father was a renowned Hebrew scholar. As a student at the University of Pennsylvania, Chomsky read linguistics, mathematics and philosophy. He was greatly influenced by the radical views of Zellig Harris, who was teaching at the University at that time. In the early 1950s, Chomsky joined Harvard as a Junior Fellow in philosophy, where Roman Jakobson was teaching. In 1955, he was given a teaching post at the Massachusetts Institute of Technology, and he has remained there ever since. Chomsky's importance lies in the fact that he has recalled the study of **language universals**, which, for many was very unfashionable and outdated. But Chomsky emphasised that unlike in the past, there should not be an effort to find out common components for all languages under the study of language universals, but to look for a grammatical framework which will be suitable for all languages. He suggested that there is a pool from which each language picks different elements, and which each language combines in different ways. Therefore, the linguist's primary aim is to discover the universal bounds within which the human language operates. Chomsky has divided the universals into substantive universals and formal universals. His substantive universals relate to the substance out of which language is made. But his formal universals concern the overall shape or form of a grammar and the way in which the various components of the grammar relate to one another. He suggests that the grammars of all languages share a common framework, which he calls a **transformational grammar**, which we shall discuss in subsequent chapters. The innovative ideas of Chomsky has put linguistics at the forefront of other social and behavioural sciences not only in the United States of America but also in other countries of the world.

GLOTTOCHRONOLOGY AND LEXICOSTATISTICS

While structural linguistics almost replaced historical linguistics or comparative philology in the beginning of this century, the importance of the study of the origin and development of languages was not undermined. This resulted in further advances in comparative linguistics in the form of bridging the gap in the methods of traditional historical linguistics. Historical linguistics, no doubt, could tell us which two languages are related to one another, but it could not confirm *how* close the given languages are. In other words, it was deficient in suggesting the precise time when two or more languages got separated from the original stock. Anthropologists, historical linguists and archaeologists are always interested in knowing at what date linguistic changes took place and how the language developments correlate with cultural changes, migrations etc., the evidence for which is available from other sources. In order to answer these problems and to provide more precise dating for the convergence or divergence of language, a new technique was devised in early 1950s, which is popularly known as **lexicostatistics**. Its significance lies at the application of mathematical techniques within the broad purview of historical or comparative linguistics to reconstruct the family tree for a group of languages, using information about the present-day languages of the family. While the term lexicostatistics denotes any of the various methods which reconstruct the family tree, **glottochronology** is reserved for those which additionally provided dates for branching points in the language family tree.

Lexicostatistics is based upon four assumptions. According to Gudschinsky, the assumptions are : (1) Some parts of the vocabulary of any language are less subject to change than other parts, which Sapir calls the basic nucleus of morphological structure; (2) The rate of retention of vocabulary in the basic core is constant through time; (3) The rate of loss of basic vocabulary is approximately the same in all languages; and (4) If the percentages of true cognates within the core vocabulary is known for any pair of languages, the length of time of their divergence can be computed, provided they are not intervened by migrations, conquests, or other social contacts. The following steps are then followed to apply the lexicostatistical techniques: (a) collection of comparable word list from the relatively stable core vocabulary; (b) determining the probable cognates; (c) computing the time depth by the formula

$$t = \log C/(2 \log r),$$

where t = time depth in millennia, C = the per cent of cognates, r = the constant or the index, that is the per cent of cognates assumed to be constant after a thousand years of divergence; (d) computing the range of error by the formula

$$\sigma \text{ (sigma)} = \sqrt{C\,(1 - C)/n}$$

where σ is the standard error, C = per cent of cognates and n = number of pairs of words compared; and (d) operationally, computing the dips (degrees of lexical relationship) by the formula

$$d = 14 \ (\log C/2 \log r).$$

The lexicostatistical data thus computed suggest the order of the development of languages and dialects, along with implying the geographical location and cultural contacts of the ancient dialects (Swadesh, 1950: 164-167: Gudschinsky, 1964: 612-622). Although there have been some important studies in this direction, the conclusions are still much contested.

4

STRUCTURE OF HUMAN COMMUNICATION

NON-VERBAL HUMAN COMMUNICATION

Human communication is a subtle blend of spoken language and a variety of extra-linguistic messages conveyed and received by all the sensory apparatus of the human body. The power of verbal articulation is certainly immense. But sometimes, non-verbal acts may also be used as a substitute for language, or they may accompany and modify the language, enriching and energising it.

The significance of gestures, facial expressions, postures and tone of voice has been recognised since classical times, when Greek and Roman scholars codified these components of oratory. In India, the art of non-verbal expression was well-researched sometime between the 4th and 1st century B.C., as we see them codified in Bharata's *Natyashastra*. Bharata has left for us many dance poses or *mudras* which express human emotion in a subtle way, without necessarily using the spoken form of language. This is also true for many classical dance forms all over the world, where gesture is the medium of expressing emotions. However, non-verbal communication became an established area of linguistic research during the 19th century with publications on conversational niceties and became 'scientific' with the incorporation of experiments and rigorous documentation—using charts, graphs, formulae, sketches etc. to record varieties of hand gestures, facial movements etc. in oratory and dance routines. Indeed, non-verbal communication is an integral part of our communicative behaviour. Whistling, hissing murmuring, finger gesturing, bowing, sitting with crossed legs and many other non-verbal communications very well indicate the anger, happiness, frustration, greeting, command, love, hatred and other feelings, which could also be expressed by spoken languages.

Thus, non-verbal expression deserves our attention in linguistics study and analysis. In this section, we shall consider some of the modes of non-verbal human communication, which either substitute or supplement the spoken languages in the normal network of human communication.

Paralinguistics

Paralinguistics is concerned with the association between certain vocal patterns and emotional expressions, in much the same way as facial expressions and emotions have been presumed to have an innate relationship. Paralanguage includes all extra speech sounds, such as, hissing, shushing whistling, imitation sounds, as well as a large variety of speech modification, such as, quality of voice (sepulchral, whiny, giggling), very high pitch, or hesitations, and rate of talking. Although many of the scientific advances in paralinguistics research among primates including man came in the 1950s, the idea of a possible relationship between nonsemantic aspects of speech and expression of emotion goes back to the writings of Charles Darwin. In noting that the calls of animals can often be tied to specific situations (for example, courtship, conflict etc.), and presumably specific emotions as well, he suggested possible evolutionary continuity in the vocal usage of humans (Darwin, 1965: 83 - 93). However, Darwin was not able to propose any coherent theory of the evolution of sound usage, and concluded: ". . .the whole subject of the differences of the sounds produced under different states of the mind is so obscure that I have succeeded in throwing hardly any light on it; and the remarks which I have made have but little significance" (*ibid*: 93). Since the time of Darwin, many advances have been made in the study of paralinguistics with the help of sophisticated machines. It has developed in two major directions: voice as an indicator of personality, and voice as the indicator of the state of human interaction. But both areas depend on the voice as a conveyor of emotion.

Kinesics

The term 'Kinesics' was introduced in the 1950s to designate the articulation of the body, or movements resulting from muscular and skeletal shift in the process of communication. This includes all actions, physical or physiological, automatic reflexes, posture, facial expressions, gestures, and other kinds of body movements. It was Birdwhistell who first became interested in body movements while undertaking anthropological field work in 1946 among the Kutenai Indians of Western Canada. Beginning in 1952, he began to propose models for the organisation of kinesic behaviour, but considering the verbal and non-verbal aspects together. As a true anthropologist in spirit, Birdwhistell favours a contextual approach to studying the entire communication situation and opposes the isolation and manipulation of variables advocated by some of his contemporaries, who are most often named as the proponents of the clinical approach to the study of kinesics.

Proxemics

Nonverbal behaviours which use space as their channel of communication can be linked together and termed as proximity behaviours. Although space cannot be seen in the same way as facial expression or body movement, or a tone of voice be heard, it is undoubtedly a vital part of every social encounter. Like kinesics, the study of proxemics is also rooted in anthropology. Edward Hall's publication, *The Hidden Dimension* in 1966 marked the beginning of the systematic investigation into the study of cultural space. Hall defines proxemics as the study of man's perception and use of space. He adds, "It is much closer. . . .to the behavioural complex of activities and their derivatives known to the ethologists as territoriality. It deals primarily with out-of-awareness distance-setting. . ." (Hall, 1968: 83). His major contributions are the delineation of four social distances, such as, intimate, personal, social, and public, which seem to be present in all cultures. Hall discusses the use of space in five cultures, namely, Germany, England, France, Japan and the Arab countries, and ties national character to the use of space. He observes that Germans are particularly orderly about marking off spatial boundaries and enforcing them, and says, "The door is taken very seriously by Germans. . .to close the door preserves the integrity of the room and provides a protective boundary between people" (Hall, 1966: 127). His observation on Japanese perception of space is that the concept of centre is an organising principle. Hall's proxemics however should not be confused with the concept of 'personal space', which is more psychological and deals chiefly with the meaning of space to the individual in terms of the effects of crowding, territoriality, architectural design, and so on, and not so much with intercultural variation. Similar to space, the understanding about the human communication in time has led to another area of non-verbal communication, which is known as **chronemics**.

American Sign Language (ASL)

We concluded in an earlier chapter that one of the most remarkable differences between man and other non-human animals is that man is uniquely endowed with the speech faculty, so that he can express different shades of meaning with the help of language. But we often observe that deaf children cannot speak. The question then becomes, whether deaf children are equally capable of acquiring and creating language to express themselves as efficiently as normal children do? In fact, it is not essential that human language be only expressed with the help of sounds. The hand and body movements of the deaf carry definite meanings, and deaf 'speakers' are capable of creating new sentences in their own gestural way, like the normal children do. The deaf children learn the sign language, if that is the language used around them, exactly in the same way as the normal children learn to speak in their own linguistic environment. Deaf children who grow up in American homes, acquire what is known as American Sign Language or AMESLAN, or ASL in abbreviated form. It is estimated that ASL is the third most commonly used non-English language in the United States.

Historically, ASL developed from the French Sign Language used in a Paris school founded in the 18th century. In the beginning of the 19th century, one of the teachers from this school, named Laurent Clerc, was brought to the U.S.A. by Thomas Gallaudet. Clerc not only taught deaf children, but trained other teachers also in the United States, and ASL gradually evolved. ASL, however, is different from British Sign Language or BSL, because of the incorporation of the features of the indigenous natural sign languages used by the American deaf. ASL is mostly based on four key aspects of visual information. These are usually classified as shape, orientation, location and movement of the hands and the palms. The shape of the hand may be either flat hand, fist hand, cupped hand etc. to convey different messages. The orientation of the hand may be with palm-up, palm-down, palm towards signer etc. The location of the hand may be at chin, waist, and movement of the hand may be upward or downward etc. In addition to these, there are many non-manual components involved in the ASL, such as, head movement, eye movement, and many other facial expressions such as, raising the eyebrows, widened eyes, leaning forward of the head, and so on. Sometimes, the expression is with the help of finger spelling also, in addition to the use of signs. Different countries have evolved different sign languages according to their very definite linguistic requirements, which millions of the deaf people use to express themselves easily and efficiently. Even news bulletins are being broadcast for the hearing impaired viewers of television with the help of sign language.

VERBAL COMMUNICATION

When we hear a parrot calling by name to us or to somebody else, we immediately understand what exactly the parrot intends to say. But we are almost sure that the parrot itself does not understand most of what it says. Similarly, when we hear two speakers communicating in an unfamiliar language and one of them speaking something in a high pitch tone, we tend to guess that the person is angry or annoyed. From these examples, it is evident that language is a two-way process involving both production and reception of sounds. As far as speech is concerned, the process involves associating sounds with meaning and meaning with sounds. This is different from writing, where meaning is associated with sign or a visual symbol. Therefore, the study of language requires the appraisal of all the levels shown in Figure 4.1 below, which provides a structure to the process of human communication.

Language

↓

Phonology	—	(sounds)
↕		
Morphology	—	(meaningful combination of sounds)
↕		
Syntax	—	(meaningful combination of words)
↕		
Semantics	—	(meaning)

Fig. 4.1: Structure of Verbal Communication

It is clear from the above presentation that in order to understand language, we need to know how sound is produced, how these are meaningfully combined to form words, how words are combined to form sentences, and how meaning is attached to words and sentences. Therefore, phonology, morphology, syntax and semantics constitute the basics of what we call the language. We shall briefly discuss each one of them, which are full-fledged sciences in themselves, in this section.

Phonology

Phonology is the study of sounds. But phonology is further divided into two different branches. One of them is known as **phonetics**, which studies the production, transmission and reception of speech sounds; the other one being **phonemics**, dealing with the study of sound and sound patterns of a specific language. Phonetics is again of different types. If we study the mechanism of production or 'articulation' of sounds, it is called **articulatory phonetics**, on which we shall concentrate in this section. The study of physical properties of the sounds themselves is called **acoustic phonetics**, and the study of the perception of speech sounds, via the ear, is known as **auditory phonetics**.

The main organs of speech, as you may see in the Fig. 4.2, are the jaws, the lips the teeth, the teeth ridge (commonly known as alveolar ridge), the tongue, the hard palate (the roof of the oral cavity), the soft palate (also known as velum), the uvula, the pharynx, the larynx and the vocal cords. The tongue is so important in the production of sound that it has been divided into four areas, the tip, the blade (or lamina), the front and the back, which help in the production of different speech sounds.

Sounds could not occur without air. Most of the sounds are produced by pushing out air from the lungs through the oral or nasal cavity, and hence, these sounds are called pulmonic sounds. Since the movement of the diaphragm pushes *out* the air, these are called egressive. Therefore, the mechanism through which we produce or articulate English speech sounds is commonly known as **pulmonary egressive airstream mechanism.** Many other languages have **ingressive** sounds produced by sucking in the air instead of pushing out, which, we shall not be able to discuss here beyond a few examples.

If we observe carefully, we will find that we produce many interesting types of sounds. Some of the sounds may be called **voiceless** sounds, while others are **voiced**; and while some are **oral**

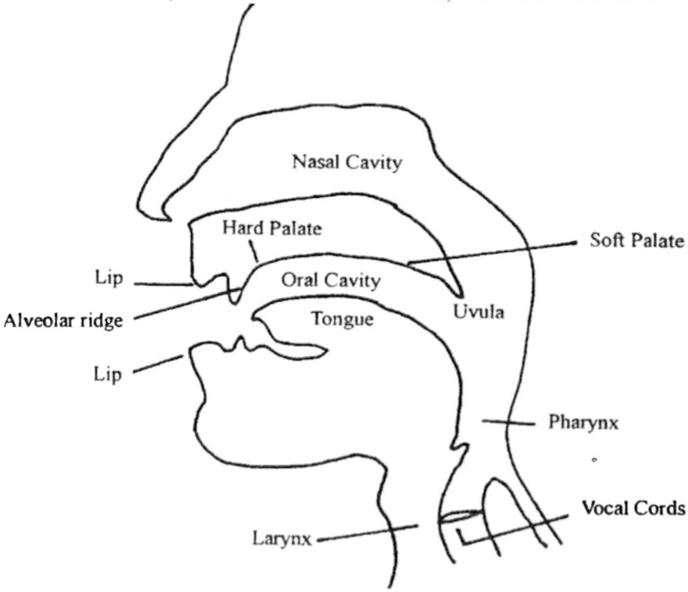

Fig. 4.2 : The Organs of Speech

sounds, some others are **nasal**. Let us now examine the mechanism behind the production of different sounds. In fact, when the air moves from the lungs, it moves up through wind pipe or **trachea** and then, through the opening between the vocal cords or the **glottis**. When the vocal cords are open, the airstream is not obstructed, and smoothly passes into the supraglottal cavities to produce voiceless sounds. Note that /p/, /t/, /k/, /s/ are such voiceless sounds, which are produced in this way. But when the vocal cords are together, the airstream has to push open the glottis, thus causing a vibration, and voiced sounds are produced. For example, /b/, /d/, /z/ sounds are produced by this mechanism, which are voiced. When you close both of your ear openings with the fingers or put your hand on your throat, and utter voiced sounds, you can distinctly feel the vibrations in your glottis. *Pin* and *bin*, *tin* and *din*, *seal* and *zeal* etc. make very distinct sets of voiceless and voiced sounds in English. Similarly, we can also distinguish between oral and nasal sounds. Take the example of /m/, /n/ and / ŋ (ng) sounds. When you compare between *bat* and *mat*, *dot* and *not*, *dig* and *ding*, you may notice that when you produce /m/ or /n/, the air not only escapes through your oral cavity, but also a part of it through the nasal cavity and the nostrils. How does the air then goes into the nasal cavity ? If you insert your index finger into the mouth and move backwards to the soft palate, you will notice **uvula** at the end of the soft palate or velum. When you produce an oral sound, the uvula is raised to touch the back of the throat by blocking the nasal passage, and hence, the air comes through the oral cavity. But when you produce a nasal sound, the velum is lowered, giving way to a part of the air to pass through the nasal cavity as well. These phonetic features enable us to classify the speech sounds of English into four classes, and the following Table 4.1 helps us to identify them:

TABLE 4.1 : Classes of Speech Sounds

	Oral	*Nasal*
Voiced	b, d, g.	m, n, ŋ (ng)
Voiceless	p, t, k	All nasal consonants in English are voiced

Although /b/ and /d/ are both voiced sounds, they are distinct in themselves, so that we are able to distinguish between *ball* and *doll*. Therefore, there are other phonetic features, besides those already discussed, that differentiate the speech sounds. In fact, depending on the *manners of articulation* and *places of ariticulation*, the voiced and voiceless, and the oral and nasal sounds can be further analysed, which we shall see in the following paragraphs with reference to English consonants.

Stops

These are the sounds produced when the airflow is completely blocked off in the oral cavity. Stops may be of the following types:

Voiceless bilabial stop : These sounds are produced when the airflow is blocked off by the complete closure of both the lips. Examine the sound /p/ in the word *pin*.

Voiced bilabial stop : When the articulation is exactly as above, but the sound is voiced, we get these kinds of sounds. For example, /b/ in the word *bin*.

Voiceless alveolar stop : These sounds are produced when the tip of the tongue touches the alveolar ridge behind the upper teeth. For example, the sound /t/ in the word *tin*.

Voiced alveolar stop : When the articulation is the same except that the sound is voiced, these sounds are produced. For example, /d/ in the word *dad*.

Voiceless velar stop : While producing these sounds, the tongue is raised and touches the soft palate or the velum. Consider the sound /k/ in the word *kind*, which is of this type.

Voiced velar stop : The manner and place of articulation is exactly the same, but a voiced sound like /g/ in the word *gag* comes under this type.

Glottal stop : While producing the sound / ʔ in the words like *button* and *Latin*, the air is stopped completely at the glottis because of the closed vocal cords. This sound is called a glottal stop.

Fricatives

These are the sounds produced when the airstream is not completely stopped as in the case of the 'stops', but is obstructed from flowing freely from the mouth. This is because a narrow passage is created in the oral cavity for the air to pass out, and some friction is created due to the narrowness of the passage. The friction can be best observed by putting the hand or a small piece of paper before the mouth. Let us examine, how different kinds of fricatives are articulated.

Voiceless labiodental fricative : The lower lip and the upper teeth are involved in the production of these sounds, as for example, /f/ in the word *fine*.

Voiced labiodental fricative : When the manner of articulation is like the above, except that the sound is voiced, we get these sounds. For example /v/ in the word *vine*.

Voiceless interdental fricative : These sounds are produced when a friction is created by the air that forces out between the tip of the tongue and the upper teeth. If we say /θ/ or 'th' as in *thin* or *theeta*, note that the air gushes out in between the tip of the tongue and the upper teeth, and the resultant vibration produces the interdental fricative.

Voiced interdental fricative : This is again the voiced variant of the above sound, represented by / ð / or 'd' as in the words *then, this* and *that*.

Voiceless alveolar fricative : When the airstream passes through the narrow opening between the tip of the tongue and the alveolar ridge, these kinds of sounds are produced. For example, the sound /s/ in the word *sit* is a voiceless alveolar fricative.

Voiced alvelar fricative : The sound /z/ in the word *zebra* is only a voiced form of the sound /s/ as we have seen in the last example.

Voiceless alveopalatal fricative : In the production of sounds like /š/ as in the word *ship*, the tip of the tongue moves up to the back of the alveolar ridge towards the hard palate, and the air passes through the tip of the tongue and the roof of the mouth causing friction.

Voiced alveopalatal fricative : The sound /ž/ as in the middle of the words like *measure* or *decision* is produced in exactly the same fashion as above, except that it is voiced.

Glottal fricative : The /h/ sound in the words *how* or *here* is often called a glottal fricative, as the vocal cords are positioned to partially obstruct the airflow from the lungs. However, the turbulence is created at different points of the vocal tract, which are determined by the vowel that follows the sound /h/.

Affricates

Some sounds are produced initially by the obstruction of the airflow as in case of stops, followed immediately by slow release of the air as in case of the fricatives. These sounds are called affricates. One can notice the following kinds of affricates in English consonants:

Voiceless alveopalatal affricate : This sound can be produced when the tip of the tongue touches the alveolar ridge or just behind it. An example is the sound /č/ in the word *church*. It may be noticed that the production of this sound is similar to that of /š/, except that the airflow is initially stopped and then released slowly.

Voiced alveopalatal affricate : The sound /ǰ/ in the word *judge* is produced in a similar fashion as /č/ or *ch*, except that it is a voiced sound.

The fricative /s/, /z/, /š/, /ž/ and the affricates /č/ and /ǰ/ are together called as SIBILANTS, as they produce a typical hissing noise.

Liquids

There are some more sounds which are produced with some obstacle to the airflow in the mouth, but which is not sufficient or strong enough to cause friction. The air eventually flows easily and smoothly. Let us consider the following types of liquids

Lateral alveolar liquid : In the production of the sound /l/ in the word *life* the tongue blade is raised and the tip touches the alveolar ridge. The sides of the tongue are lowered to allow the air to flow out.

Nonlateral alveolar liquid : This sound is produced with the tongue blade raised to touch the alveolar ridge, and many speakers curl the apex of the tongue back into a *retroflex* position. Most often, due to the retraction of the tongue root, this sound causes throat constriction. The sound /r/ in the word *right* may be taken as an example.

Glides

Glides are sometimes referred to as *semivowels* because of their vowel-like articulation. In the production of these sounds, the air flows very smoothly, as we shall see in case of the vowels. The following are different kinds of glides :

Palatal glide : When we produce the sound /y/ in the word *yes* the body of the tongue is arched in a high front position towards the hard palate, and the airflow is quite smooth.

Labiovelar glide : The sound /w/ as in the words *which* and *witch* can be produced both by raising the back of the tongue towards the velum and rounding of the lips. The first word in the example is a voiceless one, while the second one is voiced.

TABLE 4.2 : **Phonetic Symbol for English Consonants**

	Bilabial	*Labiodental*	*Interdental*	*Alveolar*	*Palatal*	*Velar*	*Labiovelar*	*Glottal*
Stop	p,b			t,d		k,g		ʔ
Fricative		f,v	θ, ð	s, z	š, ž			h
Affricate					č, ǰ			
Liquid				l,r				
Glide					y		w	

From the above discussions we observed that English consonants are produced either by total or partial obstruction of the vocal tract and eventual vibrations. On the other hand, English vowels are produced with the vocal tract relatively open, which acts as a resonator. However, the position of the tongue, opening between the lips, position of the jaw etc. determine the production of various vowel sounds, about which we shall discuss below. Vowels in English may be of three major types, such as, short or lax, reduced, and long or tense, depending upon their duration and the amount of muscular action involved in the production of the sound.

Short or Lax Vowels

Short vowels are relatively shorter in duration and involve less of muscular action. But depending on the position of the tongue in the mouth, there are different types of short vowels, as will be clear from the following discussion

Short high front vowel : In the production of the sound /I/ as in the word *bit* or /bIt/, it may be noticed that the position of the tongue is high and frontal in the mouth, and hence, the name of the vowel.

Short mid front vowel : When the tongue position is frontal but slightly lowered, this vowel is produced, as in the case of the sound /ɛ/ in the words *get* (gɛt) or *mɛs* (mɛs).

Short low front vowel : When the tongue is in the forward position, but the blade of the tongue is almost on the floor of the mouth, these vowels can be produced. Take the example of the sound /æ/ as in the word *bat* (bæt), which is a short low front vowel.

Short high back vowel : In the production of this vowel, the back of the tongue moves upward towards the velum. The sound /U/ in the words *put* (pUt) or *foot* (fUt) may be taken as the example. The lips also get rounded in the production of this sound.

Short mid back vowel : When we pronounce the sound / ∂ / in the word *caught* (c ∂ t), we are necessarily producing a short mid back vowel, when the tongue movement is associated with minor lip rounding.

Short low back vowel : When the position of the tongue is low and retracted, we produce the sound /a/ as in the words *hot* (hat) and *pot* (pat), which is the representative of this vowel.

Short central low vowel : This is represented by the vowel sound /^/ in the words like, *luck (l^k)* or *bus* (b^s), where the tongue blade touches the floor of the mouth.

Reduced Vowels

There are two reduced vowels in English, which we shall discuss below.

Reduced high central vowel : This is represented by the symbol /ɨ/, which is commonly referred to as barred-i. This is the second syllable of the word *chicken* or /č I k ɨn /. This vowel occurs only as an unstressed syllable in the word.

Reduced mid central vowel : This is represented by the symbol / ∂ /, which is in the form of upside down and reversed /e/. It is the last vowel of the word *sofa* of /sof /. It is also commonly unstressed as in the case of the reduced high central vowel. The following table presents various short and reduced vowels in a tabular form:

TABLE 4.3 : **Short and Reduced English Vowels**

	Front	*Central*	*Back*
High	ɪ	ɨ	ʊ
Mid	ɛ	ə	ə
Low	æ	^	a

The long vowels differ from the short vowels, as these are not only longer but also sound higher than the short ones. Further, the long vowels in English usually have two parts; an initial louder vowel, followed by a less loud vowel. Because of having two parts, these long vowels are otherwise known as **diphthongs**. Let us look at the following examples to understand this.

Long high front vowel : This is represented by the symbol /iy/ in the word *bead* or /biyd/. One can notice the length of the sound here and its two parts. The sound of the second component, that is /y, is difficult to hear, as it is articulated in the same position as the initial /i/.

Long mid front vowel : This is represented by the sound /ey/ in the word *weigh, clay* etc.

Long low front vowel : The sound /a w/ in the words *bout* (ba wt) may be grouped under this, and its length and composition confirming to diphthong could be easily noticed.

Long high back rounded vowel : This is represented by the sound /uw/ in the word *shoe* (suw). Another feature of this sound is the lip rounding while articulating the sound /uw/.

Long mid back rounded vowel : This vowel is represented by the sounds /ow/ and /oy/ in the words *boat* (bowt) and *boy* (boy) respectively; the lip rounding in their articulation being evident.

Long low back vowel : This is again represented by two sounds, /aw/ and /ay/ in the words *cow* (kaw) and *my* (may) respectively.

TABLE 4.4 : **Long or Tense Vowels**

	Front	*Back*
High	iy	uw
Mid	ey	ow, oy
Low	æw	aw, ay

Phones and Allophones

Sometimes phonemes have different phonetic variants depending on its position in the syllable or morpheme. These positional variants of a given phoneme are known as its **allophones.** Discovering these allophones or positional variants of the phonemes in a language is indeed a challenging task for anthropologists, as they most often deal with unwritten languages. Let us take an example to understand this. In English, the phoneme /p/ is expressed with many positional variants depending on its position in a word. When it occurs at the beginning of the word, it is pronounced with aspiration (with a puff of air coming from the mouth). But the same phoneme /p/ is articulated without aspiration, if its position is after /s/. This becomes very clear when we pronounce the words *pot* and *spot*, or *pill* and *spill*. Here then, the sound /p/ has two variants; an unaspirated /p/ and an aspirated /pʰ/, and /pʰ/ is an allophone of the phoneme /p/. All phonemes, however, do not vary equally and therefore, the amount of variation differs from phoneme to phoneme. For example, slight variations in the pronunciation of /s/ are almost unperceptible and unimportant, whereas the variations of /l/ is easily noticed. When the variation in the pronunciation is accepted and goes unnoticed, the allophones are said to be in **free variation**. If the final consonant /t/ in the word *kit* is pronounced either as /kʰIt/ or /kʰI:? t/, for example, the variation goes unnoticed and the distinction between the allophones /t/ and / ? t/ is not regarded as contrastive. But the case is not the same in the difference between *pot* and *spot*, where the allophones /p/ and /pʰ/ cannot substitute each other. Therefore, when two allophones occur in a position where other allophone(s) can never occur, and vice versa, they are said to be in **complementary distribution**. So long as the phones or sounds do not contrast among themselves, they remain as the allophones of the phoneme, either in complementary distribution or in free variation.

Morphology

We noticed in the preceding section that sounds in themselves are not really important, unless these are meaningfully combined to form what we call 'words' in a language. These words represent the form of the language concerned. But words which appear as one, may be constituted by one or more than one smaller components. Let us take the example of the word *boyish*. Although this is one word it has two meaningful and grammatical components, boy and -ish. Similarly, in the word *desirability*, there are three grammatically significant components, such as, desire, -able, and -ity. These basic elements in the form of linguistic messages are technically known as **morphemes**, and an investigation into the form of any language is termed as **morphology**. The word 'morphology' is used in biology for the study of the form of the organism, which is derived from the Greek word *morphe* (meaning form). Since the mid-19th century, 'morphology' has also been used in linguistics to understand the form of the language. Let us now consider the nature of morphemes, which are otherwise "the minimal units of meaning or grammatical function", and are not further divisible.

Free and Bound Morphemes

Morphemes may be of two different types. There are many **free** morphemes, which can stand by themselves as single words without any attachment. For example, *boy, man, dog, tree, and, but, when, because, on, near, above* and many others. Free morphemes are further divided into two types, such as **lexical** morphemes, which are ordinary nouns, adjectives and verbs like *boy, man* etc. in the above example, which carry the content of the messages that the speaker wants to convey. But there are also other examples like *and, but, when* etc., which are basically functional words in a language like conjunctions, prepositions, articles, pronouns etc., and are known as **functional** morphemes. Besides the free morphemes, there is also another group of morphemes, known as **bound** morphemes, which cannot normally stand alone like the free morphemes and therefore are typically attached to another form. Many *prefixes* and *suffixes* that we use as a part of our language are nothing but the bound morphemes, which are by themselves meaningless. Let us take the example of -er in the word *singer* or-ist in the word *Marxist*, which convey nothing without being attached to the free morphemes like sing or Marx respectively. Bound morphemes are however of two different types. There is a group of **derivational** morphemes among them, which are used to make either a new word or a word of a different grammatical category from the stem. For example, the morpheme -ness in the word *kindness* changes the stem from its adjective form to a noun form. Similarly, the morpheme -ment in the word *payment* very clearly changes a verb into a noun. Prefixes like re-, pre-, ex-, dis-, co-, un- and others also belong to this category. The second set of bound morphemes are known as **inflectional** morphemes, which do not produce new words, but certainly indicate change in the grammatical function of the stem. Let us consider the morphemes -ed in the word *jumped* or -ing in the word *singing* or -s in the word *girls*, which belong to this group. Interestingly, all inflectional morphemes in English are suffixes.

There are many languages other than English, which use *infixes* more often to change the grammatical form of the stem. One such example has been presented by Fromkin and Rodman (1978) from the Bontoc language spoken in the Philippines, where the infix, -um is inserted after the first consonant of the noun or adjective for transforming the word into its verb form.

Nouns/ Adjectives	*Verbs*
fikas (strong)	f*um*ikas (to be strong)
kilad (red)	k*um*ilad (to be red)
fusul (enemy)	f*um*usul (to be an enemy)

The following chart presents the categories of morpheme that we have discussed above:

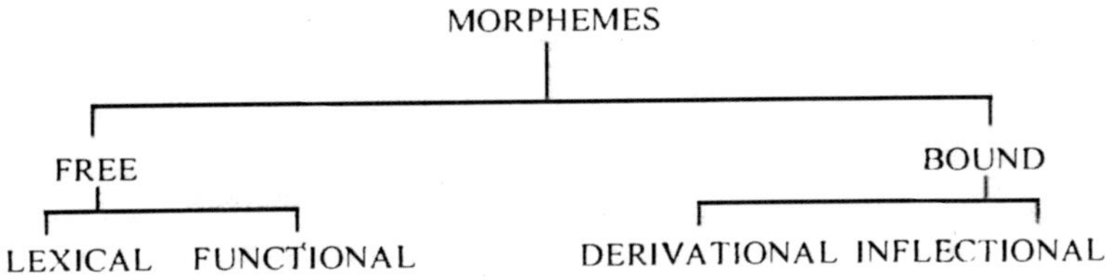

Fig. 4.3 : Types of Morphemes

With the help of this classification, we should now be able to list the elements of or attempt a morphological description of, the sentence. Let us then consider the sentence: *The girl's kindness impressed the teachers,* which has the following elements:

The	*girl*	*-'s*	*kind*	*-ness*
(functional)	(lexical)	(inflectional)	(lexical)	(derivational)

impress	*-ed*	*the*	*teach*	*-er*	*-s*
(lexical)	(inflectional)	(functional)	(lexical)	(derivational)	(inflectional)

Morphs and Allomorphs

Just as there are allophones of a particular phone, a morpheme may have a number of variants. These are known as **allomorphs** of the concerned morpheme. In other words, when a morpheme has alternate phonetic forms, these forms are the allomorphs of that morpheme. Let us take the example of the plural morpheme. Predictably, -s, -z and -Iz are the allomorphs of the regular plural morpheme. While -s occurs after most voiceless phonemes as in *cats* or *giraffes*, -z occurs after most of the voiced phonemes, such as, *dogs, bees, lambs* etc., Iz, however, usually occurs after the sibilants (hissing and hushing sounds) as in words *horses, dishes* etc. But how to understand the plural forms like *sheep, geese, oxen, men* etc.? This has been resolved by recognising that zero-morph is also an allomorph of the plural, which takes care of the word *sheep* by saying that the plural form of sheep is sheep + 0. Other forms are said to have individual morphological realisation rules like ox + plural. The same rule is also applicable to some forms of past tense, like go + past tense.

Syntax

When we attempt to study the structure and ordering of components within a sentence, we are studying what is technically known as the **syntax** of a given language. In fact, the word syntax comes originally from Greek and means 'arrangement'. Literally, therefore, syntax is the analysis of arrangement of words within the sentence. We know that merely putting a few unrelated words in a row does not make up a meaningful and grammatically correct sentence. There are certain very definite and stringent underlying rules needed to arrange words to present a correct sentence. In this chapter, we shall dwell on the ways in which words are linked together to form larger units, and perhaps more importantly, discuss how to analyse sentences into their component parts, or **constituents** in linguistic terminology.

Most of the languages have devised their own methods to show the relationship of one word to another in a sentence. But there are some common devices as well, which are followed by almost all languages. One of these is the **word order** or the proper arrangement of words in a sentence. Let us consider the following pairs of sentences:

The black cockroach frightened Mrs. Sushma.
Mrs. Sushma frightened the black cockroach.

The words in both sentences are identical in form and number. Despite this, both the sentences convey altogether different meanings, precisely because of the arrangement of words in the sentences. The subject in the first sentence becomes the object in the second, and hence, the change in the meaning.

The second commonly used device in many languages is the use of **function words** like *of, by* etc. These are basically 'empty words', which do not indicate syntactic relationships, and do not refer to identifiable objects, qualities, or actions. This is clearly seen from the following examples

*Mrs Pratima was terrified **by** a tiger.*
*She is the Queen **of** the lost empire.*

The appropriate use of function words and the proper arrangement of words in a sentence is broadly what is called the **grammar** of a language. It is this internal linguistic knowledge which lies at the subconscious level of thought, which children master by the age of 5 years, and which helps them to express themselves unambiguously.

In **traditional grammar**, the structure of expression is analysed with the help of commonly used **parts of speech**. We are already familiar with articles, nouns, pronouns, adjectives, verbs, adverbs, prepositions and conjunctions as the constituent parts of speech. Let us again recapitulate them with help of the following sentence

The	*naughty*	*boy*	*threw*	*the*	*stone*	*at*
article	adjective	noun	verb	article	noun	preposition

the	*angry*	*tiger*	*and*	*they*	*cheered*	*loudly.*
article	adjective	noun	conjunction	pronoun	verb	adverb

In addition to the parts of speech, traditional grammar also uses a number of other categories for analysis, which include 'number'. 'person', 'tense', 'voice' and 'gender'. We already know that number may be singular or plural; person may be first, second or third; tense may be present, past or future, voice may be active or passive; and masculine, feminine or neutral. This classification although holds good for English, it is not appropriate for many other languages. For example, Sanskrit grammar has three numbers instead of two found in English. Similarly, many languages do not recognise neutral gender. The local classification varies greatly from culture to culture, and we shall discuss this in the next chapter.

The analysis of traditional grammar is approached from two directions : **prescriptive** and **descriptive**. In the 18th century England, some rules were set out for the 'proper' use of the language, which was characterised by the prescriptive approach. For example, was grammarians insisted that an infinitive must not be split, or the sentence must not end with a preposition etc. In common usage however we find the teacher correcting such sentences as : *I shall (not will) visit my grand-parents during the vacations*, or *Baby is taller than I (not me)* etc. This approach helps one to understand the 'linguistic etiquette' or the 'proper' use of the language in question, which may be called a social expectation.

The descriptive approach to the study of the structure of a language is different from the prescriptive approach in at least one fundamental way. The former does not take any model of the grammar of a language for the analysis of any other language. For example, Latin grammar may be a useful guide for the analysis of Italian or Spanish, but it cannot be of any help in the analysis of a native American language. In fact, at the end of the 19th century, there were a number of native languages found which needed to be analysed by describing the regular structure of that language, which could not be fitting into any set model. This approach came to be known as the descriptive approach to the study of language.

Sentences are not simply random words put together; instead, they follow sentence patterns. An analysis which seeks to show how the constituents of sentences fit together to form larger constituents is commonly known as **immediate constituent analysis**. In the following example, we can see how the constituents are arranged in the sentence.

'he police caught the thief in the market.

Eight words in the sentence can be divided into three phrase-like constituents. *The police* is the noun phrase (NP), *caught the thief* is the verb phrase (VP), and *in the market* is the preposition phrase (PP). Further, NP is divided into *the* (article) and *police* (noun). Similarly, VP is divided into *caught* (verb) and the *thief* (another NP, further divisible into an article and a noun). The PP is also divided into *in* (preposition) and *the market* (NP, further divisible into an article and a noun). The constituent analysis can also be presented with the help of the following **tree diagram.**

While the traditional approaches treat syntax as the study of the structure of sentences, the most influential contemporary approach to the study of syntax takes the sentence as the basic unit of analysis. This is Chomsky's **transformational-generative** (T/G) analysis, which brought about a revolution in linguistics during 1950s and had a strong impact on linguistics for a considerably long time thereafter. This uses the approach of describing languages in terms of rules for the production of sentences. Although many sentences can be formed in any language, the rules for such production which native speakers follow are surprisingly limited. Further, these rules are found to be similar in type from language to language, thus hinting at some degree of underlying similarity between languages.

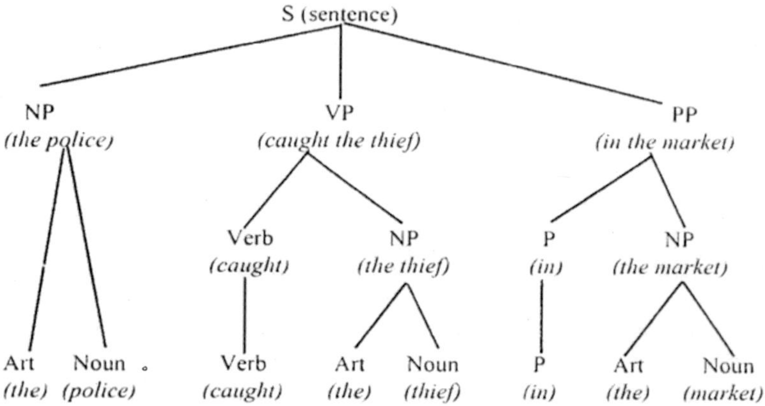

Fig. 4.4 : Tree Diagram

Chomsky's grammar is based upon several important assumptions. Chomsky considers **productivity** or **creativity** as a very important property of human language. This means the ability of human beings to produce and comprehend an indefinite number of novel utterances, which they might not have uttered before. In fact, every speaker works out for himself or herself a set of rules, quite unconsciously, which constitutes a part of his/her linguistic ability. Chomsky asserts that these internalised sets of rules are the speaker's **competence**, which the linguist should discover. He stresses that these rules are of far greater interest than the actual utterances that the speaker makes during normal conversation, to which he refers as the speaker's **performance**. Because the competence lies in the human mind, Chomsky aptly suggests that linguistics is an important branch of cognitive psychology. If we assume that the speaker has internalised some basic rules of the grammar of the language, every time he makes a new sentence, he expands the basic rules to accommodate the latter. Let us examine these basic rules, which come under **phrase structure grammar**. Such a grammar contains a series of rewrite rules which show progressive expansions, as we have seen in case of the immediate constituent analysis. In the following formulae, S represents a sentence, NP=noun phrase, VP=verb phrase, ADJ = adjective, N = noun, ADV = adverb, V = verb, AUX = auxiliary verb, and so on. The items in the brackets should be read as optional requirements. In the sentence, *The cat may eat the fish,* the phrase structure rules followed are :

S → NP + VP
NP → DET (determiner) + N
VP → VB (verb) + NP
VB → AUX (auxiliary verb) + V (main verb)
the → DET
cat, fish — N
may — AUX
eat — V

On a tree diagram, the rules appear as follows :

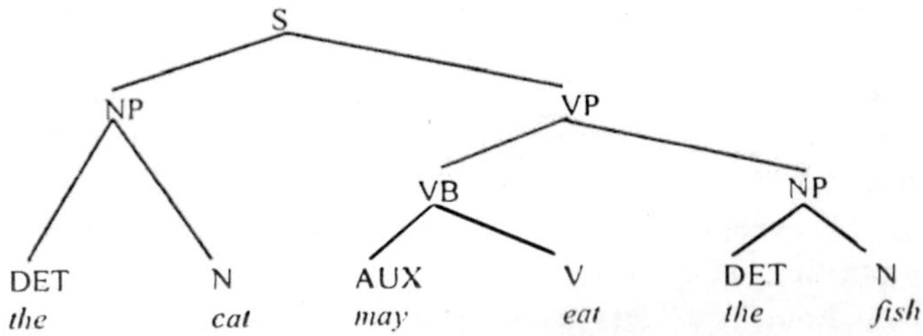

Fig. 4.5 : Tree Diagram of P-S Rules

Although these basic and preliminary rules are applied to the most simple sentences, which are able to generate an infinite number of sentences, when the sentence becomes complex, additional rules are devised in the following manner to comprehend them :

NP	→	DET + (ADJ) (adjective) + N or
NP	→	PRO (pronoun)
VP	→	V + NP + PP (preposition phrase)
PP	→	P + NP

Therefore, however long the sentence may be, it can be analysed very easily with the help of the phrase structure rules, as all of them follow these simple rules of syntax. But sometimes sentences appear within sentences, where the grammarian follows what is called the **recursive** rules. In order to understand this, let us take the example of the sentence, *He thought, he would fight till the last.* Here we find, one sentence is **embedded** or inserted into the main sentence, thus creating a condition of recursion. Recursion, however, is possible in another condition, when the sentences are **conjoined** using the conjunctions like, and, but etc. For example, the sentence, *Mary played tennis and Ahmed went fishing,* presents a recursive condition, where two sentences are conjoined or fused to make a single sentence. Recursion, therefore, is the possibility of repeatedly using the same construction, so that there is no fixed limit to the length of the sentences. The implication is, no matter what the length of the sentence, it follows some very limited phrase structure rules, which underlie the complex construction of the sentences.

Besides these phrase structure rules, which are basically generative in nature, there is also another series of rules of transformation that helps to derive negative, exclamatory, interrogative and complex sentences from simple declarative sentences. We shall examine here just one example of **reflexive transformation** as a representative of the transformational rules. In English, we have a number of reflexive pronouns, such as, myself, yourself, himself, herself, itself, ourselves, yourselves and themselves. Their distribution however is very special in the sentence. For instance, they cannot function as a subject NP like other pronouns. The sentence *Herself cursed Geeta* (Geeta cursed herself) is therefore ungrammatical. Again, if a reflexive pronoun appears in a sentence, it must have an antecedent elsewhere in the same sentence. In the sentence *Geeta cursed herself,* the antecedent of 'herself' is 'Geeta', which also appears in the same sentence to refer the reflexive pronoun. Further, the reflexive pronoun must be the NP with the same person, number and gender as the antecedent. For example, if the above example is rewritten as *Geeta cursed himself* or *John cursed herself*, the sentences become ungrammatical. Invariably, we find that if there are two identical noun phrases referring to the same individual in a sentence, the second one is substituted by a reflexive pronoun that is the same as the person, number and gender of the first. The above example could be represented by the following tree:

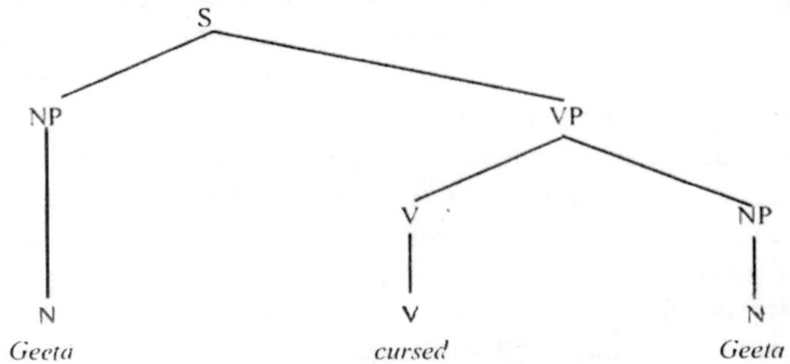

Fig. 4.6 : Tree Diagram of Transformation

The reflexive rule transforms the above phrase structure tree into the following one:

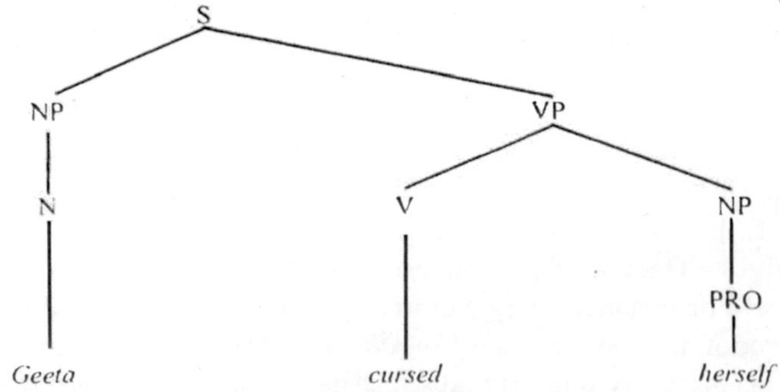

Fig. 4.7 : Reflexive Transformation

The reflexive transformation rule therefore states that "within a sentence, if there are two occurrences of identical noun phrases that refer to the same individual, replace the second with a reflexive pronoun that matches the first in person, number, and gender". The phrase structure tree that results from these analytical exercises of syntax is termed by Chomsky a **deep structure**. The deep structure is, therefore, the abstract form of a sentence, at the level of which the differences between the languages appear to be minimum or non-existent, because the relationships between the components are mostly conceptual and are governed by the innate structure of the human mind. On the other hand, the phrase structure trees that evolve on application of the transformational rules, which correspond to the actual utterance of the sentence is termed as the **surface structure**, which is the realisation of the sentence as morphemes and phonemes.

Semantics

In linguistics, semantics is generally considered to be the study of the meaning of words, phrases and sentences. Linguists are more concerned with the **conceptual** meaning of words, phrases or sentences than the **associative** or stylistic meanings when they analyse them. While the conceptual meaning refers to the essential components of meaning, the associative meaning is usually the connotation attached to the meaning of a word. As understanding the meaning is a necessary part of the linguistic competence of a speaker or a hearer, it has a vital role to play in the process of communication. Meaning, however, may be of two different types : **linguistic meaning** and **speaker's meaning** as explained in Fig. 4.8. Very broadly we can infer that linguistic meaning is conceptual, whereas speaker's meaning is associative. While the linguistic or conceptual meaning is the conventional translation of the meaning of a word, the speaker's or associative meaning is indicative of the context in which the speaker speaks. Let us examine the following examples to understand the differences between them.

*What a **beautiful** nose you have !*
*What a **beautiful** nose you have !*

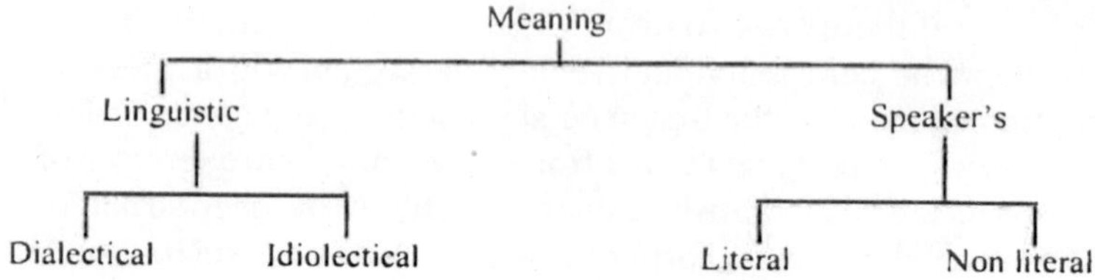

Fig. 4.8 : Types of Meaning

Both the sentences, although the same, any one of them could be used satirically or teasingly by being critical to other's nose. The other sentence could be an admiring expression of other's nose. Therefore, speaker's meaning could be just *literal* or *non-literal*, depending on the context. Non-literal uses of language may include sarcasm or irony or could be used metaphorically, as often being done by the poets and writers.

Linguistic meaning may be also of different types. Meanings may vary across dialects and between individual speakers. This implies that the same words may be used differently by people speaking different dialects of the same language, and sometimes, the meaning of the same word varies from person to person. Therefore, there may be both dialectical as well as idiolectical differences in meaning, which make the field of semantics most challenging for the linguist. It is more so for an anthropologist, who mostly studies unwritten languages.

The question which arises now is, what is meaning ? What sort of entity is it ? How is it to be understood ? Answers to all these questions have led to different conceptions of meaning, which in turn, have led to different theories of semantics. We shall discuss some of them here.

Referential Theory of Meaning

This theory states that the meaning of each expression is the actual object it refers to. For example, if names of persons or places or definite objects or descriptive noun phrases are expressed, these convey definite meanings, that is the referent of each expression. If the speaker says, for example, *the moon, Kautilya, the President of India, Professor Chomsky* etc., the hearer does not have much of problem in understanding the referents with respect to each of these expressions. But there are certain inherent problems in this conceptualisation. For example, expressions like *the, hello, empty* have meanings without reference to actual objects. Similarly, the referential theory is questioned when it states : if two expressions have the same referent, the meaning of both of them is the same. For instance, *the morning star, the evening star, and venus* refer to the same object. but they do not mean the same thing. Therefore, referential theory is not an absolutely satisfactory theory of meaning.

Mentalist Theory of Meaning

This theory proposes that meanings are not actual objects, but are mental objects, and hence, refer to an idea or ideas associated with the expressions in the speaker's mind. This solves problems like ascertaining the meaning of words like *love, empty, innocence* etc. but faces some other serious difficulties. First of all, the notion of an idea is too vague to predict anything specific and it is not testable. We have examined some examples while discussing literal and non literal meanings, where an expression could be used metaphorically or satirically as well. From its external appearance, or in its written form, it is difficult to subject these ideas or concepts or feelings to any kind of test to find out their exact referents. Therefore, the mentalist theory is also found to be unsatisfactory to understand meaning.

Use Theory of Meaning

The use theory of meaning was proposed by Wittgenstein in 1930s, and states that the meaning of an expression is determined by its use in a particular language community. In a given language community the speaker's meaning of an expression is more or less standardised, and hence, the hearer does not have much difficulty in understanding the meaning. Because of a shared process of language acquisition and the sharing of a normative pattern of behaviour, the meaning does not become obscure for the hearer. However, in this theory, the conception of use must be made precise, so that it leaves no room for confusion about the relationship between meaning and use.

Lexical Relations

Meanings are not only associated with the words that contain them, but are also in mutual relationship between words. Therefore, meanings could be derived either conceptually or relationally. In the semantic description of a language, linguists also analyse the relationship between words, which is commonly known as lexical relations. In this section, we shall discuss some of these lexical relations, which are very commonly understood and used.

Synonymy

Two or more forms are said to be synonyms, when they have very closely related meanings, which are very often but not necessarily always, used as each other's substitutes in the sentences. Examples are: *apathetic/passive/ indifferent* or *pedigree/ancestry/descent* and so on. It should be however remembered that there are no perfect synonyms or words with exactly the same meanings, as the contextual use of the words are basically different.

Antonymy

Words which are opposite in meaning are often called antonyms. The common examples of the antonymous pairs are: *male/female, hot/cold, young/old* and many more of them. Antonyms are usually divided into two sets. The first is named as **gradable** antonyms, which are used in comparative constructions, and the negative of one of the pair does not necessarily mean the other. Let us look at this example : *The man is not old*. This does not necessarily mean that the man is *young*, as young/old are antonyms. The second kind is called **non-gradable** antonyms or complimentary pairs, which are normally not used in comparative constructions, and the negative of one of the pair necessarily implies the other. For example, *He is not dead* certainly implies that *He is alive*. Similarly, *male/female, true/false, married/ single* etc. are non-gradable antonyms.

Hyponymy

When two or more words are in a hierarchical relationship, and the meaning of one is included in the meaning of the other, the words are said to be hyponymous to each other. For example, *rose/flower, cow/animal, cabbage/vegetable* and so on. In these examples, as rose is a *flower, cow* is an *animal*, and *cabbage* is a *vegetable*, the meanings of *flower, animal* and *vegetable* are included in the meanings of *rose, cow* and *cabbage* respectively. Moreover, the components of each of these pairs are placed hierarchically among each other. In this hierarchical relationship, if more than one word come under the same super ordinate term, the former are **co-hyponymous** to each other, such as, *rose/lily/chrysanthemum* (all being *flowers*), *cow/goat/sheep* (all being *animals*), and *cabbage/potato/carrot* (all being *vegetables*).

Homophony, homonymy and polysemy

When two or more different written forms have the same pronunciation, they are termed homophones, such as, *flour/floor, to/two, meat/meet* etc. On the other hand, words with the same written and spoken form but with very unrelated meanings are said to be homonyms. Some of the common examples of homonyms are: *bank/bank* (one referring to the bank of a river, and the other meaning an institution), *pupil/pupil* (one meaning a student, and the other to the organ in the eye), *mole/mole* (one indicating a mark on the skin, and the other meaning an animal) etc. Polysemy however refers to identical words with related multiple meanings due to the extension of one meaning to another. In the pairs of words, *head/head,* one refers to the head of a body and the other one refers to the head of an institution. Here, the meanings are related to each other, although these are used in different contexts. Similarly, *run/run* are polysemous to each other, as both refer to the movement or flow of either a person or water.

Metonymy

When two or more words manifest a very close connection between each other like a container-contents relationship or a whole-part relationship or a representative-symbol relationship, they are said to be metonymous to each other. For example, *bottle/wine, house/verandah* and *Governor/Raj Bhavan* represent each of the above categories respectively. These are simply based on a close connection in everyday experience. In fact there are so many such words which are highly conventionalised and used in our day to day conversation.

5

LANGUAGE AND CULTURAL ANALYSIS

In the early part of the 19th century, the German scholar, Wilhelm von Humboldt (1767-1835), wrote, "The spiritual traits and the structure of the language of a people are so intimately blended that, given either of the two, one should be able to derive the other from it to the fullest extent. . . .Language is the outward manifestation of the spirit of people : their language is their spirit, and their sprit is their language; it is difficult to imagine any two things more identical". Modern anthropological studies, however, have revealed that there is no explicit relationship between language, culture and race, as many closely related cultures have different languages, and many different cultures speak similar languages. The classic examples, perhaps, are the Dravidian language, Brahui, spoken in Pakistan, and the distinct Mundari and Dravidian speakers in the hills of Central India in the same habitat. Boas, in his introduction to *Handbook of American Indian Languages* (1911) rejected any intrinsic relationship between a people's physical type, culture and language. Sapir largely endorsed the view of Boas about possible disjunction between language and culture, but nevertheless believed that ". . .language and our thought-grooves are inextricably interwoven, (and) are, in a sense, one and the same" (Sapir, 1921: 228, 232). In fact, he believed that language influenced its speakers to a very significant extent. His contention was "Though language is not ordinarily thought of as of essential interest to the students of social science, it powerfully conditions all our thinking about social problems and processes. Human beings do not live in the objective world alone, nor alone in the world of social activity as ordinarily understood, but are very much at the mercy of the particular language which has become the medium of expression for their society. . . . The fact of the matter is that the 'real world' is to a large extent unconsciously built up on the language habits of the group" (Sapir, 1929: 209).

Sapir is of the opinion that language is an essential tool in the reconstruction of cultural chronologies, particularly in cultures without any historical or archaeological record. He contends that of cultural and linguistic changes, the latter comes more slowly and evenly. Since language is more compact and self-contained, and free from the conscious rationalization of the speakers, even after major social revolutions, language is relatively less changed than society or culture. In his book, *Time Perspective in Aboriginal American Culture* (1916), he cites many examples from his native American studies to show how language might be used as a key to the understanding of the cultural history of a society. However, his most provocative statement, that humans are at the 'mercy' of their languages, was at the centre of controversy and inspired some young anthropologists to look for the possible relationship between language and culture. Among many of Sapir's students, it was Benjamin Lee Whorf (1897-1941), who expanded Sapir's ideas and expounded what is commonly referred to as the Sapir-Whorf hypothesis, or more appropriately, the Whorf hypothesis on language and world view, which we shall discuss below.

LANGUAGE AND WORLD VIEW

In this section, we shall discuss the Sapir-Whorf hypothesis or more appropriately, the **Whorf hypothesis** on the relationship between language and world view. Sapir and Whorf particularly drew attention from linguists and anthropologists because their thought contrasted with many of the American descriptivists. Although they fully shared the linguistic relativism of Boas and other descriptivists, they were not impressed by behaviourism of the most powerful and influential Boasian successor, Leonard Bloomfield. Sapir, for example, believed that "Language. . . .not only refers to experience largely acquired without its help but actually defines experience for us by reason of its formal completeness and because of our unconscious projection of its implicit expectations into the field of experience. . . .Such categories as number, gender, case, tense,. . . .are not so much discovered in experience as imposed upon it because of the tyrannical hold that linguistic form has upon our orientation in the world" (Sapir, 1931

209). Because of this quite radical approach, Sapir and his student, Whorf, claimed rather a separate place among the American anthropologists.

Benjamin Lee Whorf was, as aptly remarked by Sampson, an outstanding example of a brilliant amateur. Whorf, a chemical engineer by training, was a fire prevention inspector and then an executive of a New England fire insurance company in the U.S.A. till his premature death in 1941, at the age of 44. In the year 1931, Whorf enrolled at Yale University in order to do graduate study under Sapir. He was influenced by the ideas of Sapir and continued to probe into the relationship between language and culture. Expanding on Sapir's ideas, Whorf proposed that "...the background linguistic system (referring to the grammar) of each language is not merely a reproducing instrument for voicing ideas but rather is itself the shaper of ideas. ... We dissect nature along lines laid down by our native languages. . . .organize it into concepts, and ascribe significances as we do, largely because we are parties to an agreement to organize it in this way—an agreement that holds throughout our speech community and is codified in the patterns of our language....(Not) all observers are....led by the same physical evidence to the same picture of the universe, unless their linguistic backgrounds are similar (Whorf, 1940: 231). In another context, Whorf said that ". . . .users of markedly different grammars are pointed by their grammars toward different types of observations. . . .and hence are not equivalent as observers but must arrive at somewhat different views of the world" (Whorf, 1940a: 61). Thus, Whorf puts a dualistic principle before us; the first being the principle of *linguistic determinism* that the way one thinks is determined by language, and second, the principle of *linguistic relativity* that differences among languages are reflected in the world views of their speakers.

In order to substantiate his argument on the relationship between language and world view. Whorf cites some examples which he encountered in his profession in the insurance company. For instance, Whorf tells us, people usually behave cautiously near 'full petrol drums' but indifferently, if they are marked 'empty petrol drums'. This causes more accidents because even the 'empty' drums contain explosive petrol vapour and hence, are more dangerous than the full drums. Similarly, 'spun limestone' is more often dealt without much precaution causing fire hazard, as the people believe that 'stone' is basically incombustible. Through these examples, Whorf tried to strengthen his assertion of the relationship between language and world view, although the bulk of his data came from his study of the Hopi language of Arizona in the U.S.A. He compared Hopi with what he called 'SAE' or Standard Average European languages (consisting of English, German, French and so on), trying to find out the broad areas of meaning in different languages. His interest centered round the questions of whether the concepts of 'time', 'space' and 'matter' were the same in all languages or were conditioned by the structure of particular languages. Further, he tried to find out the possible affinities between cultural and behavioural norms and large-scale linguistic patterns.

Whorf tries to prove that the concept of time is different in Hopi and SAE as expressed in the languages. For example, he says, SAE can form both "real" and "imaginary" plurals like *ten men* and *ten days*. While 'ten men' is a real plural which can be seen and counted, 'ten days' is an imaginary plural which cannot be objectively experienced. Here Whorf argues that in SAE there is a tendency towards 'objectification' of time, as if it can be measured. On the other hand, he says, Hopi does not have imaginary plurals, as the concept of his time is cyclical and cannot be measured objectively. Therefore, Hopi does not borrow 'spatial' terms to refer to 'temporal' phenomena as is commonly found in European languages. Furthermore, Whorf says that Hopi verbs do not have tenses like SAE languages. Hopi verbs are, rather marked by validity forms which indicate whether the speaker reports, expects or speaks from his previous knowledge about the situation. Whorf, therefore, contends that while the SAE microcosm sees the world in terms of 'things' and imposes spatial forms on non-spatial aspects of existence, contrarily, the Hopi "seems to have analyzed reality in terms of events. . .".

Despite its meticulous arguments, Whorf's hypothesis has been subjected to many criticisms. For example, Max Black (1959) objects to Whorf's interpretation of Hopi thought by saying that his claim is untestable and vacuous. He suggests that Hopi might have the same concept of time as we have, but their way of saying is different from ours. Similarly, Salzman (1993) establishes through examples from Arapaho kinship terminology that since the Arapaho has same term for 'my mother' and 'my mother's sister' (*nei:oo*) this does not mean that the Arapaho does not conceptually distinguish between the biological mother and her sister (p. 158). He further objects to Whorf's hypothesis by citing the example of Chinese lexicon where the same form of noun stands for both the singular and the plural. "Yet the lack of marked grammatical number in nouns and hence no need to differentiate between one or more entities has obviously not prevented the Chinese from making achievements in mathematics and science" (Salzmann, 1993: 160). It is like saying that if any language does not have a word 'bus', this certainly does not prevent its speakers to recognise one when they happen to see it. Considering all these, I think, Sampson very aptly remarks that "So long as Sapir and Whorf claim only that our mother tongue provides an arbitrary but convenient set of pigeonholes for categorising experience, on which we tend to rely whenever it appears to matter little what particular scheme of categorisation we use, they are surely right. No doubt they are right, too, to argue that the decisions which we allow our language to pre-empt in this way sometimes matter more than we realise. But when they suggest that we are helpless prisoners of the categorisation scheme implied by our language, Sapir and Whorf underestimate the ability that individual men possess to break conceptual fetters which other men have forged" (Sampson, 1980: 102).

When we move away from the Whorfian monotony of identifying parallels between the general grammatical categories of language and the 'logic' of culture, which is very difficult to prove, we can still find specific relationships between culture and lexicon. Franz Boas in his classic study of the central Eskimo of Canada in 1883-1884 and in the introduction to the *Handbook of American Indian Languages* has cited many such examples. He writes that in Eskimo language, ". . . .the SEAL in different conditions is expressed by a variety of terms. One word is the general term for SEAL; another one signifies the SEAL BASKING IN THE SUN;

a third one, a SEAL FLOATING ON A PIECE OF ICE; not to mention many names for the seals of different ages and for the male and female" (quoted in Hickerson, 1980: 108). Hickerson also mentions Evans-Pritchard's classic study among the Sudanese Nuer in the 1930s and the linguistic reflexes of their relationship with cattle and the pastoral ideology. Evans-Pritchard observed that "He who lives among the Nuer and wishes to understand their social life must first master a vocabulary referring to cattle and the life of the herds" (1940). The Nuer identify 10 principal colour terms, 27 terms for various combinations of colours, and special terms for rare combinations of more than two colours for their cattle. Besides these, there are metaphorical names for cattle on the basis of their resemblances with leopard or python or guinea-fowl etc. Further, There are 6 different terms for various configurations of horns, besides terms for the age and sex of the cattle population. Not only the sphere of terminology but the totality of the Nuer cultural life and its orientation around their cattle has been fascinatingly described by Evans-Pritchard. Cattle in marriage payments, as sacrificial objects for appeasing to and communicating with the ghosts of the dead, as the basis of Nuer cycle of annual calendar, as the source of naming children etc. reveal the Nuer perception of the world through their cattle.

The limited influence of grammatical features of a language on the pattern of behaviour has been used by some anthropologists to decipher the nature of the relationship between language and culture. One study of this kind was undertaken by Carroll and Casagrande among the Navaho of the U.S.A. The authors conclude that a Navajo speaker invariably chooses from among several forms of verbs of handling according to the shape or some other characteristic of the object being handled—for example, solid roundish (rock), slender and flexible (rope), flat and flexible (cloth), slender and stiff (stick), noncompact (wool) and so on (Salzmann, 1993: 160). This habit of verb selection operates at the level of unconscious awareness of the speaker, and even a child of three or four years does not make a mistake in this regard. Their comparison between the predominantly Navajo speaking and predominantly English speaking Navajo children reveals that "The tendency of a child to match objects on the basis of form or material rather than size or colour increases with age and may be enhanced by. . .learning to speak a language, like Navaho, which because of the central role played by form and material in its grammatical structure, requires the learner to make certain discriminations of form and material in the earlier stages of language learning in order to make himself understood at all" (Carrol and Casagrande quoted in Salzmann, 1993: 161).

ETHNOSCIENCE AND COGNITIVE ANTHROPOLOGY

In order to study the relationship between language, culture and cognition, several closely related approaches developed in the late 1950s. Although most of these approaches are designated by the widely used common name of **ethnoscience**, they include cognitive anthropology, ethnosemantics, formal analysis, ethnolinguistics, folk taxonomy, componential analysis, new ethnography and many others. Ethnoscience or cognitive anthropology ". . . .is the study of the relation between human society and human thought. The cognitive anthropologist studies how people in social groups conceive of and think about the objects and events which make up their world— including everything from physical objects like wild plants to abstract events like social justice. Such a project is closely linked to psychology because the study of how particular social groups categorize and reason inevitably leads to questions about the basic nature of such cognitive processes" (D'Andrade, 1995: 1).

The approaches involved in ethnoscience and cognitive anthropology are by no means new. One can find some sort of continuity between them and the writings of earlier anthropologists like, Radcliffe-Brown, Lévi-Strauss, Nadel, Mauss, Boas, Sapir and Bateson etc. There are, however, some sharp contrasts in the aims, assumptions, goals, and methods between the earlier anthropological formulations and ethnoscience. The earlier theoretical orientations were either concerned with the problem of change and development or with static descriptions. While evolutionism and diffusionism dealt primarily with patterns of change and progress, functionalism contemplated exclusively on the functional relationship between different culture traits and their contribution towards the maintenance of the culture as a whole. The ultimate aim of these endeavours was to construct universal organizational types either by similar process of change or by similar internal structure, as evidenced from the evolutionary and functional perspectives respectively. But the problem was that every time there was empirical information that did not quite fit the theoretical paradigms which were supposed to be universally generalizable. This led to the proliferation of types, thus defeating the original intention of proposing highly generalizable theories. Anthropology, therefore, became more particularistic rather than generalized as expected. With the quest for universal patterns of culture, there was a further problem of incorporating the atypical data that did not match the proposed theoretical models. Either these otherwise valuable data were simply dismissed as pathological types or were expressed as indices of change, survival, innovation, dysfunction etc.

"In contrast to these approaches, cognitive anthropology constitutes a new theoretical orientation. It focuses on *discovering* how different peoples organize and use their cultures. This is not so much a search for some generalised unit of behavioural analysis as it is an attempt to understand the *organizingprinciples ofunderlying* behaviour. It is assumed that each people has a unique system for perceiving and organizing material phenomena—things, events, behaviour, and emotions (Goodenough, 1957). The object of study is not these material phenomena themselves, but the way they are organized in the minds of men" (Tyler, 1969: 3, italics in original). The significant departure of cognitive anthropology from earlier anthropological theories is that it does not intend to analyse culture as a bunch of material phenomena, but the way these material phenomena are organized in human minds. It also rigidly advocates the use of an **emic** rather than **etic** approach to utilize the usefulness of native perceptions of categorization, and thereby rule out any possibility of imposition of the researcher's own prejudice on the final analysis of the native culture. The anthropologist, therefore, depend on the information shared by the natives, and should not interpret the data himself.

Tyler proposes that cognitive anthropology should seek to answer two fundamental questions: (1) What material phenomena are significant for the people of a given culture ?, and (2) How the people of the given culture organize these phenomena in their unique ways? This obviously implies that the importance of material phenomena considerably varies from culture to culture, and hence, differential cognitive organization of these phenomena in different cultures. This means that the same phenomenon might be perceived differently in different cultures, which makes each culture unique and independent of others. Tyler aptly argues that the subtle differentiation between dew, fog, ice and snow for an American is of little significance to the Koyas of South India, who call all these variants with the common name of *mancu*. Similarly, all the seven varieties of bamboo appear to be redundant to an American, who knows all of them as one. Further, the differences between different cousins with their associated social duties and obligations among the Koyas do not make much sense for the Americans, for whom cousins constitute one single kinship category. Therefore, what is important in this approach is to reflect on the mental organization of different phenomena in a given culture, rather than to understand culture as a mere assemblage of these phenomena. Tyler concludes, therefore, that it is not so much a 'theory of culture' as it is 'theories of cultures'. This theory then is the conceptual model of organization provided by an adequate description of the rules that regulate the cognitive vision of the people in a culture (*ibid.*: 5).

The question that is now raised is how an anthropologist can study the mental process of ordering the phenomena by the people of a culture. Ethnoscience and cognitive anthropology lay emphasis on the language used by the people in categorizing their universe. In every culture, people classify things into different groups following the method of **taxonomy**, which in turn is bound by the twin principles of **inclusion and contrast**. This means that while items at the same level contrast with one another, items at different levels are related by the process of inclusion. Let us examine this principle by the following taxonomy used by Tyler (*ibid*: 7).

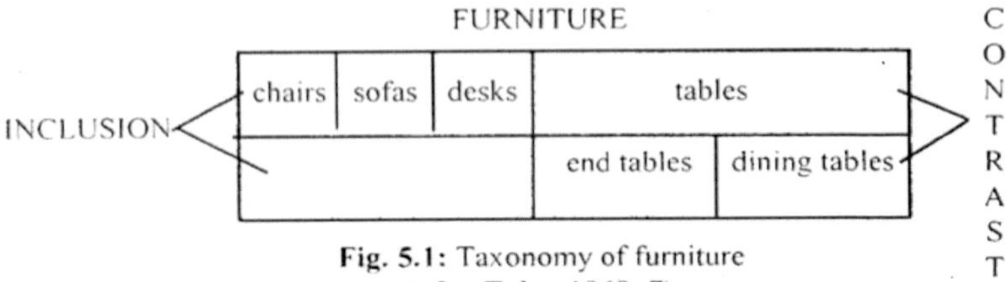

Fig. 5.1: Taxonomy of furniture
(after Tyler, 1969: 7)

The above figure is an example of a **semantic domain**, where chairs, sofas, desks and tables are all included under the common term, furnitures, as all of them share something in common. They are bound together by the principle of inclusion. On the other hand, they contrast one another as a chair is different from a sofa, and a sofa is different from a desk, and so on. Anybody having some knowledge of English does not confuse a sofa and a chair, but including them under furnitures tells us that the mental organization of different phenomena by the people of a culture could be studied with the help of the terms they use for different objects and the meanings associated with them. Cognitive anthropology, therefore, explores native categories of phenomena with the help of folk semantics, where a researcher has little room for the manipulation of data or imposing his own interpretation on the domain of folk perception.

There have been many important studies in anthropology seeking to understand and analyse the insider's view of his own culture, using the native semantics. One early study is the Hanunóo colour categories by Harold Conklin. While Conklin was conducting an extensive ethnobotanical study among the Hanunóo of the Philippines, he also collected and analysed Hanunóo colour categories in a landmark study, the findings of which were published in 1955. Conklin found that the Hanunóo colours could be divided into the following four main categories, with a prefix of *ma-*, which is the Hanunóo term for 'having' or 'exhibiting':

ma-biru	"darkness, blackness"
ma-lagti	"lightness, whiteness"
ma-rara	"redness, presence of red"
ma-latuy	"greenness, presence of green"

These native Hanunóo colour terms could be roughly translated into English as black, white, red and green respectively, which provide a four-way division of the colour spectrum which can include any shade or mixture of colours. The colour, *ma-biru* does not only refer to black, but many deep shades like dark blue, violet, green, gray and their various mixtures, stands in contrast to *ma-lagt* ? , which includes white and many very lightly pigmented shades. The other two colours, *ma-rara* ? and *ma-latuy* also contrast each other as the former stands for red, orange, yellow and their mixtures derived from dryness or desiccation in plants, while the later represents light green, light yellow, and light brown derived from freshness or succulence in plants. It is very interesting to observe that while native aesthetics place an emphasis on *ma-biru* and *ma-rara* ? the colours of *ma-lagti* and *ma-latuy* are considered to be weak, faded and colourless. The colour green is unattractive for the Hanunóo, and hence, it is not used for decoration. Although Hanunóo language can designate many more colours, these four basic colour terms provide the main framework in which colour is categorized and discussed among the Hanunóo. This line of analysis has been further carried forward by Berlin and Kay from a crosscultural perspective and a much wider scale in later times (Berlin and Kay, 1969).

Another good example of looking at a domain of another culture with the help of native categories and languages comes from Charles Frake on the folk perception of diseases among the Eastern Subanun, shifting cultivators of western Mindanao in the Philippines (Frake, 1961). Subanun frequently discuss sickness and diseases among themselves, and consequently, their language has many terms related to disease. Frake finds out that the Subanun mostly use single words for the names of the diseases, and sometimes use descriptive phrases like *mengebag gatay* for 'swollen liver'. In Subanun categorization of diseases, *nuka* (skin disease) contrasts with *samad* (wound) and *pasu* ? (burn). *Nuka* may be of many varieties, such as, *pugu* (rash), *mengebag* (inflammation), *beldut* (sore), *buni* (ringworm) among others. A *beldut* is further classified according to depth (shallow or deep), distance from the point of origin (distal or proximal), severity (severe or mild), and spread (single or multiple). Each of these variants are denoted by different terms, although for a non-native observer, the disease is one and the same. For example, Subanun disease of *telemaw glai* refers to shallow distal ulcer which is considered to be severe. The diagnosis, for Subanun, is certainly not an end in itself, rather it is a cognitive step towards the selection of culturally appropriate treatment for the illness and final selection of herbal medicines from many alternates and propitiatory offerings. The anthropological objective of this kind of meticulous analysis is to point out that "To diagnose and classify Subanun diseases from the vantage point of Western medicine may be appropriate for an article to be published in a medical journal. However, for an anthropologist such a description would fail to reveal or at-least would obscure the linkages that the Subanun believe to exist between the method of diagnosing diseases and the application of remedies to them. This is so because the final diagnosis and choice of appropriate treatment have important social and economic consequences in Subanun society" (Salzmann, 1993 : 165).

With the possibility of semantic analysis being extended to many patterned and well-defined domains of native cultures, Ward Goodenough proposed in 1956 a method to solve the problem of analysing the organization or structure of a kin term system. This method of analysis is popularly known as **componential analysis** or **distinctive feature analysis**. The method consists of an explicit step-by-step process to carry out a componential analysis of kin terms. The aim, however, is to discover the semantic distinctions that make the terms contrast with one another. For example, if we select gender and relative age from the semantic dimensions to analyse the kinship terms, grand-father would be male + and old +, whereas grand-daughter would be male— and old—, which means that these two kin terms contrast with each other on the indices of male-female and young-old. This kind of analysis finally speaks about the manner of organization kin terms in binary contrasts, which is peculiar to the culture concerned. This cultural distinctiveness of patterning the semantic variables is most clear, when we compare the English kinship terminology with many

Indian systems. For example, in English, the term cousin refers to the offspring of ego's uncle or aunt or someone descended from a grandparent etc., where the gender distinction is inconsequential. In other words, gender is not a distinctive component of English cousin term. In contrast to this, in Hindi, *bhatija* and *bhatiji* denote male and female cousins respectively. Similarly, while in American kinship terminology, the gender (or sex) of the speaker is not a distinctive variable, it is very much so in Arapaho kinship terminology (Salzmann, 1993: 166). Application of componential analysis to the native semantic universes helps an anthropologist discover the underlying semantic differences between cultures, and also to determine what is culturally significant in different societies and how the members of these societies structure their experiences linguistically in characteristically distinctive ways. Thus, ethnoscientific and cognitive anthropological studies have set an agenda of anthropological studies, wherein language is considered not merely as the means of communication, but also a rich repository of information to elicit data for complete cultural studies and analysis.

The protagonists of ethnoscience and cognitive anthropology claim that these approaches entail a rethinking of the concept of culture, the comparative method which has been in use in anthropology for quite a long time, and of ethnography in general. For them, culture has to be identified with cognition; and cultural anthropology is a **formal** science rather than a **natural** science. The former implies that culture consists of mental phenomena which can be analysed by formal methods similar to those of mathematics and logic. In other words, culture consists of a set of logical principles that order the material phenomena, and the scope of cognitive anthropology is to discover these logical principles with the help of native semantics, rather than to lay emphasis on the material phenomena of a culture. Its main aim is to penetrate beyond the material representation of a culture to the logical nexus of its underlying phenomena. It has a direct bearing on the conventional ethnography, where the data constitute discrete material phenomena only, which could be analysed like other material phenomena of the natural sciences. So far as comparative method is concerned, the cognitive anthropologists maintain that instead of identifying total cultures as the units of comparison, it is much more relevant to compare similar but not identical facts within the same system. "Comparisons between systems can only be useful, if the facts compared are truly comparable, and we cannot know what facts are comparable until the facts themselves are adequately described. When this is achieved, the units of comparison will be formal features rather than substantive variables" (Tyler, 1993: 15).

Despite its immense contribution towards the mental representation of material phenomena in different cultures, ethnoscience and cognitive anthropology have some shortcomings. Salzmann remarks that their emphasis on understanding culture through language results in the neglect of nonverbal behaviour and those aspects of culture that are outside the domains accessible through terminological sets (Salzmann, 1993: 170). Harris adds to this criticism that the ethnoscientists do not prefer to accept the cultural domains which derive their salient semantic order from ambiguity and variation, other than the domains of consensus and uniformity. Obviously, Harris has in mind such activities as poetry, art and literary criticism, eschatology, traditional philosophy and theology that are often characterized by semantic ambiguity, which by no means can be dismissed as epiphenomenal or as subcultural variations (Harris, 1968: 583). The exclusive dependence of the cognitive anthropologist on the information shared by the natives, or the reliability and authenticity or data gathered by an emic approach, has been questioned, since the particular informant has every possibility of being prejudiced or over/underestimating the information. Further, the ethnosemanticists do not mention if the final mental categories that they present (such as the colour categories or naming of diseases in the works of Conklin and Frake respectively) are unanimously endorsed by all their informants, or there are differences of opinion in varying degrees.

Some of the critics look at ethnoscience as anti-evolutionary, anti-historical and anti-comparative because of its inclination towards mentalism. Harris observes that "Ethnosemantics may be able to develop valid and, within limits, useful descriptions of contemporary social systems, but the linguistic model. . . .is inherently incapable of making discoveries about the content of history and the nature of historical processes. If anthropology is to have a diachronic component, that component cannot consist of an inventory of cognitive rules" (*ibid.*: 603-604).

To conclude, the main accomplishment of cognitive anthropology has been to portray detailed descriptions of cultural representations of different kinds with the help of semantic dimensions. Another major achievement has been to create a bridge between culture and human psychology in a different way than the earlier culture-personality studies. While the ". . . .culture and personality approach demonstrated the way socialization experiences influence personality systems which in turn influence cultural practices and beliefs; cognitive anthropology has demonstrated that the psyche is influenced by the representations it learns as part of the human cultural heritage. Cognitive anthropology has also tried to show that cultural heritage itself is influenced by the inherent capacities and limitations of the human cognitive system—that the influence between cultural representation and cognitive process is reciprocal" (D'Andrade, 1995: 252).

ETHNOGRAPHY OF COMMUNICATION

The idea of an ethnography of communication goes back to Dell Hymes, who published an article with the title, "The Ethnography of Speaking", in 1962. While reviewing several weak intellectual areas involving **speech** to which anthropology can contribute, Hymes felt that "For the anthropological study of behaviour there is another area of importance, one that seems general, central, and neglected. It can be called the *ethnography of speaking*" (Hymes in Fishman, 1968: 101; italics in original). Hymes is of the opinion that this study fills the gap between what is described in grammars of a linguistic study and what is described in an ethnographic study. While conventionally, linguists study the structural differences between languages and their historical development, anthropological or ethnographic studies revolved round the nature and function of cultures. What is of mutual interest to a linguist and an anthropologist is to recognise the inseparability of language and culture, as people must use language to accomplish a variety of culture-specific goals.

Hymes emphasizes that "In order for societies to function smoothly, their members must have not only linguistic competence (the knowledge of the grammatical rules of their mother tongue, acquired well before adulthood) but also **communicative competence**—the knowledge of what is and what is not appropriate to say in any specific cultural context" (Salzmann, 1993: 193). Therefore, for Hymes, "The ethnography of speaking is concerned with the situations and uses, the patterns and functions, of speaking as an activity in its own right" (Hymes in Fishman, *op. cit.*: 101). It would be, hence, appropriate to say that the **ethnography** of **communication** primarily focuses on those aspects of human behaviour in which culture meets communication, thus contributing to an interdisciplinary understanding of human expressive behaviour.

Fieldwork is central to ethnography of communication approaches. In outlining its importance, Hymes writes: "The reasons are several: because the phenomena are there, ready to be brought into order, so that systematic descriptions can give rise to a comparative study of the cross-cultural variations in a major mode of human behaviour (a "comparative speaking" besides comparative religion, comparative law, and the like), and give it its place in theory; for the contribution to other kinds of concern, such as studies of the formation of personality in early years" (*ibid.*: 102). Therefore, although it aims at describing and understanding communicative behaviour in specific cultural settings, it is also directed towards the formulation of concepts and theories that could contribute to the global theory of human communication.

The ethnography of communication focuses on the **speech community** as its unit of study. It endeavours to understand ". . . .the way communication within it is patterned and organized as systems of communicative events; and the ways in which these interact with all other systems of culture" (Saville-Troike, 1989: 3). What is, then, a speech community ? It certainly does not coincide with a society or a culture, where language is never spoken uniformly by all members. The spoken language varies a great deal within the same society differentiating men from women, young from the old, poor from the rich, and so on. Even within the small geographical space of a village or a town, spoken language varies, considerably, depending upon many social and linguistic criteria. Therefore, "All those who share specific rules for speaking and interpreting speech and at least one speech variety belong to a **speech community**" (Salzmann, *op. cit.*: 194).

In order to understand different units or levels of communicative or speech behaviour, Hymes makes use of three different terms for its description and ethnographic analysis. These are: **speech situation, speech event,** and **speech act** (Hymes, 1972: 56-57). A **speech situation** is the context or the circumstances in which the speaking takes place. For example, it is possible during a family dinner, community meeting, seminar and symposium, fair and festival, hunting expedition, at a bathing ghat, and a large number of such situations that take place in a society everyday. Each speech situation is different from the others with regard to the type of participants and the objectives behind it. This implicitly determines the nature of communicative behaviour, which is characteristically different from situation to situation. Needless to say, speech behaviour during a community feast would not be the same as during a hunting or a fishing expedition. A **speech act** may be considered as the minimal unit of speech for an anthropological analysis. This may be expressed by greeting, compliment, approval or disapproval, question, apology, and so on. The speaker(s) of the speech act may be an individual or a group. The latter may be found in religious congregations, school prayer meetings, and the like. The speech act may vary in its size from a single word, like 'thanks' or 'excellent', to a long sentence or a story. When these speech acts, which are the basic units of verbal interaction, are arranged in a recognised sequence and are governed by the social rules of a given society, they constitute, what Hymes calls, a **speech event**. Examples of speech events include intense conversation, interview, dialogue with another person, enquiry over telephone and so on. The boundary between successive speech events may be drawn by the change in the composition of participants, an intermittent silence, or a deliberate remark to change the topic of conversation to a new one etc. However, under some special circumstances, a speech act may become a speech event, for example, when someone shouts "Fire!" in a place of public gathering like in a cinema hall (Salzmann, *op. cit.*: 196). It may be remembered that just as the speakers of a language are expected to speak grammatically correct and meaningful sentences, so are they expected to produce speech acts which must be appropriate to specific situations or speech events. If the speaker does not fulfil this condition, his speech is considered to be out of context, or he may be thought silly or abnormal in extreme cases.

Hymes observes that any speech event can be seen as comprising several components, and ethnography of speaking strives to analyse these components. He provides about **seven** such components: a sender (or addresser), a receiver (addressee), a message form, a channel, a code, a topic, and setting (scene, situation). For further discussion, we should combine the sender and the receiver together as participants. Who then are the **participants** in a communicative event and what is its **setting**? Ordinarily, we suppose that communication is between the humans, and more specifically, between the speaker and the hearer(s). But in some cultures, communication is not confined to humans only. It may be extended to other components of nature, including the plants and animals. But a still different practice could be found among the Ashanti of West Africa, when "....a midwife may direct to a foetus concerning its father's identity, and recently deceased persons are believed to be able to inform their surviving relatives as to who or what was responsible for their death. The Ashanti also believe that forest fairies and monsters are able to instruct young men in medicine; these beings are said to communicate in a whistle language but are able to understand Twi, the language in which humans pray to them" (*ibid.*: 196). When the participants are humans, one can even notice the differences in communication depending on the age, sex ethnicity, social status and so on of the participants . It is not only the participants that are important in the ethnography of communication, but also the setting, which has again a cultural variation. While joking between two kin persons bound by joking relationships is easily acceptable under normal situations; it is taken seriously when there is a death or a misfortune in the family. Similarly, although practical jokes are acceptable on April Fools' Day, it is certainly considered presumptuous on any other day.

Most commonly, the **channel** used for human communication is **acoustic**, through which message is conveyed orally. But it is well-known that there are many other channels of communication which again vary cross-culturally. Quite commonly, one channel may be used as a substitute of another. For example, "The military salute, using the optical channel, substitutes a visual expression of respect or honour for what could otherwise be orally recited. . ."(*ibid.*: 198). Sometimes a photograph or a piece of art best substitutes the oral expression. Ethnography of speaking, therefore, aims at analysing both the acoustic and non-acoustic channels of communication and their cultural variations.

Hymes suggests that the **code** factor in a language is variable and depends on the speech habits of a population. Human language is expressed through a large number of specific codes, which are otherwise classified as languages. Each code may be further subdivided into dialects on the basis of the regional or local variation of the spoken language. In fact, Hymes notes, "It is clear the status of a form of speech as a dialect, or language, or level, cannot be determined from linguistic features alone, nor can the categories be so defined. There is a socio-cultural dimension. . . .. and the indigenous categories must be discovered, together with their defining attributes and the import of using one or another in a situation" (Hymes in Fishman, *op.cit.*: 112). The Ashanti data presented by Salzmann may be considered as the best example of the socio-cultural use of codes in communication. Although Twi is the principal verbal code of the Ashanti, the ritual language used by the priests and priestesses is not intelligible to the common men of the community. Similarly, the ghost language can only be understood by unborn babies and toothless infants. Other nonverbal codes of the Ashanti include a drum code to convey messages; the gong code for public summons; whistling of the forest fairies and monsters to instruct the medicinemen etc. (Salzmann, *op. cit.*: 198-199). Cross-cultural variation could be easily noticed in the use of such codes for communication among the members of the speech community and between them.

The **form** of a message, Hymes asserts, is a descriptive fact which assumes importance as an aesthetic and a stylistic matter, in relation to the resources of a code, to a particular context, or to a particular referential content. The **topic** factor, on the other hand, addresses to the study of the lexical hierarchy of the languages, including idioms and the content of the utterances. The form and content of the message are, however, closely related to each other, and hence, Hymes states, "It is a truism. . . .that *how* something is said is part of *what* is said" (Hymes 1972: 59). As a result, we may find a variety of language to suit a particular social situation, commonly known in American linguistics as **register** (Salzmann, *op.cit.*: 199).

The **method** used in studying the ethnography of communication is primarily intense fieldwork in another culture or in one's own, which includes participant observation, interview, and the eventual validation of one's perceptions against the institutions of the researched community. The research ought to be so designed as to allow an openness to categories and modes of thought and behaviour of the speech community under study. To study and understand the pattern of behaviour in a different speech community which is largely unconscious and culturally unique, and comparing it with one's own, gives the ethnographer a sense of cultural relativism. Although total escape from subjectivity is not assured in this method because of the nature of the subjects, the constraints and guidelines of its methodology are intended to minimise the perceptual and analytical bias of the researcher (Saville-Troike, 1989: 4).

Ethnography of communication has considerable **significance** for anthropology. It ". . . .extends understandings of cultural systems to language, at the same time relating language to social organization, role-relationships, values and beliefs, and other shared patterns of knowledge and behaviour which are transmitted from generation to generation in the process of socialization/enculturation. Further, it contributes to the study of cultural maintenance and change, including various acculturation phenomena in contact situations, and may provide important clues to culture history" (*ibid.*: 8). So far, the scope of ethnography of communication has been almost exclusively synchronic and descriptive, which necessitates more and more cross-cultural comparisons of the social uses of speech. Besides Hymes' original formulation, the field of ethnography of communication is subsequently enriched by the contributions of John Gumperz, Dan Slobin, Richard Bauman, Susan Philips, Susan Ervin-Tripp, Ben Blount, Muriel Saville-Troike among others.

6

SOCIAL AND SPATIAL CONTEXT OF LANGUAGE USE

LANGUAGE VARIATION

It is an undeniable truth that the language varies with its speaker. Notwithstanding many similarities between their respective ways of speaking, no two speakers of the same language speak in an identical way. While modern linguistics is mostly concerned with the pattern of the language commonly shared by its speakers, the focus on the aspects of variation of speaking that distinguish one speaker from another is relatively marginalised. But both these aspects contribute equally significantly to the understanding of a language; hence, de Saussure distinguishes between *langue* and *parole*. The study of language variation is a fascinating and developing subfield of linguistics, which is known as **sociolinguistics**. Sociolinguistics specifically looks at speech variation in its social context. As the speakers do not only differ from each other as individuals, but also on the basis of their age, sex, ethnicity, religion, class, caste, place of residence, occupation and so on, it is quite common to come across speech variation. Therefore, sociolinguistics is concerned with the correlation between various social factors and speech variation.

The Speech Community

The basic unit of analysis in sociolinguistics is the **speech community**, rather than the more diffusely defined language. A speech community is the social unit in which the speakers ". . . .share a set of rules for using and interpreting speech in all the special settings, nuances, and cultural meanings unique to a particular community. The speech community may include one or several languages; it is localized cross cutting the wider distribution of national and world languages" (Hickerson, 1980: 81). Despite many definitions of the speech community attempted by sociolinguists from time to time, many practical difficulties in delineating it still remain unresolved. For example, do the British and the English speaking Indians belong to one speech community ? Similarly, do the French, Spanish, Portuguese speaking populations in many parts of the world qualify as speech communities with the people of France, Spain and Portugal ? In a different context, whether speakers of mutually unintelligible dialects of Chinese belong to the same speech community, as they claim to be ? All these and other related problems notwithstanding, the relative degree of sharing rules and usages of language among a group of speakers with mutual communicative capability may be taken as the criterion for delimiting the boundaries of different speech communities.

Idiolects, Dialects, and Styles

As has already been stated, every individual has a distinct style of speaking. This for example, has made it easier to recognise familiar voices on the telephone, even though the speaker does not reveal his identity. Similarly, unfamiliar voices are easily recognisable, and hence, further query follows. The voice of a popular newsreader or an announcer or an advertiser on the television can also be easily recognised without watching the screen, as the speech of an individual is characteristically unique. This is possible due to an idiosyncratic mixture of voice quality, pronunciation and preferential usage of words by an individual speaker. Since the voice quality of an individual is determined by the anatomy of the vocal tract over which he does not have much control, his speech stands out as different from any other to a large extent. This is, however, not to say that the voice quality of a speaker does not change at all in his life time. When he grows older or is affected by diseases of the vocal tract, the quality of the voice automatically changes like all other biological processes. This variation of an individual's speech variety is commonly referred to as **idiolect**. But all individual speakers again use several idiolects as they speak on different occasions and in various circumstances. For example, an individual speaking in his sitting room to the members of his family will speak differently from the way he speaks as an announcer or advertiser at the television studio where he works. Again, the way a politician speaks at a political meeting will be different from the way he speaks to his wife or children at home. Therefore, the concept of idiolect refers to a very specific phenomenon, namely the speech variety, used by an individual. When we try to find out something common from the idiolects of a group of individuals by means of abstraction, we get a **dialect.** The term dialect, therefore, refers to a form of language or speech used by the members of a social or ethnic or regional group, having something in common. By implication, hence, dialect is spoken by a small localised group of individuals, which is intelligible to all its members, and is considered to be an intelligible variation of the same language. Most often, dialects do not have scripts of their own and use the common scripts of the language. Although in practical situations, it is difficult to draw the exact boundary between the individuals speaking allied dialects within one linguistic zone, they serve as good analytical categories to account for speech variations.

Regional variations in the use of dialects could be presented with the help of a linguistic atlas. Usually, individual linguistic terms are considered to be separate between different zones that use them. For example, if a majority of the informants in one area say that the major means of transportation of goods by road is by *lorry* and the people in a neighbouring area say it is by *truck*, then it is quite possible to draw a line on a map dividing these two areas as different with respect to the use of a particular linguistic term. This line is known as an **isogloss**. When a linguist draws a number of such isoglosses on a map and they overlap indicating a thick solid line, it indicates a **dialect boundary**.

It has been mentioned earlier that speech variation does not only depend upon the place of habitation of an individual or his social standing in his society, but also according to the context in which he speaks. The special manner in which people speak in particular situations is referred to as a **style**. As appropriate dresses are required in very specific situations, such as, wedding dress, mourning dress, war dress and so on, so speech styles are also required on different occasions. Formal and informal situations demand stylistic variations of speech, and any deviation from this is considered to be 'bad manners' on the part of the speaker.

Stylistic variations of speech are not only lexical, but also phonological, morphological and syntactic as well. A stylistic or dialectical variety of speech which is formal, used by political leaders and the upper socio-economic classes, used for literature or printed documents, taught in the schools, used in mass media etc. often takes the place of a dominant dialect, and is commonly referred to as a **standard dialect**. For example, standard British English is used in prestigious English public schools, heard during radio and television newscasts, and used in formal occasions like in lectures, sermons etc., while its many stylistic variations could be heard in less formal situations. A standard dialect, therefore, serves more of a social function, which does not necessarily mean that it is in anyway linguistically superior or more expressive or more logical or better than any other dialect. Its popularity or superiority could only be judged by using purely social considerations.

Register and Jargon

Variation of the dialect according to use in very specific situations is studied in terms of **register**, and therefore, for example, we have religious, legal and other professional registers. The significance of the registers is that the expressions found there may not be found elsewhere. For example, the expressions *Ye shall be blessed by Him in times of tribulation* or *The plaintiff is ready to take the witness stand* are typical to religious and legal registers respectively, and are found there exclusively. As we find in the above examples, what makes the registers so special is their use of special **jargons**. Jargon is ". . . .defined as technical vocabulary associated with a special activity or group. In social terms, jargon helps to connect those who see themselves as *insiders* in some way and to exclude *outsiders*" (Yule, 1996: 245; italics mine). Since every specialised trade or profession uses its own jargon, their respective registers bear a special significance.

ASPECTS OF SOCIO-LINGUISTICS

Social Class and Dialectical Variation

The socio-economic status of a person reflected in pronunciation indicates the relationship between social class and variation in speech sound. For example, Labov (1972) looked at the dialectical variation between salespersons in three city department stores in New York, Saks, Macy's and Klein's belonging to high, middle and low status respectively. Labov was particularly interested in the pronunciation (or not) of the /r/ sound after the vowel, and asked the sales persons questions that elicited the expression, *fourth floor*. He found a regular pattern in pronunciation, such as, the higher the socio-economic status, the more /r/ sounds, and the lower the socio-economic status, the fewer /r/ sounds were produced. A similar study in Reading, England by Trudgill (1974), however, produced an opposite result, as the upper-middle class English speakers tended to pronounce less /r/ sounds compared to their lower/working class counterparts. This indicates differential social values associated with the same pronunciation in different places. Nevertheless, the occurrence of more /n/ sound like *talkin'* and *speakin'* etc. are more associated with lower social class throughout the English-speaking world, instead of /ŋ/ sound at the end of the words as in *walking* and *waiting*, which indicates the pronunciation of a higher social class. The dropping of /h/ sound in the word like *'ello* is another social marker, which indicated lower social status and less education of the speaker in contemporary English, adequately reflected in the writings of Charles Dickens in the middle of the 19th Century (Yule, 1996: 241).

Age, Sex, and Dialectical Variation

Age of a speaker even within the same social class more often determines speech variation. This difference can be easily noticed among the people belonging to alternate generations, such as between grand-parents and grand-children. The use of words like, *biscope, icebox, wireless* etc. and the general speech accent used by members of the grand-parent's generation are often considered as unfashionable by younger speakers.

There have been many studies of the correlation between gender and speech variation. John Fischer (1958), for example, noticed that more use of *-ing* (as reading, searching) at the word ending characterised female speech, the frequent use of *-in* (as readin' and searchin') was associated with the male speech, when he interviewed a group of school children of both the sexes. The former is often considered to be more formal than the latter. But 21 out of 24 children alternated frequently between both forms during the interview. Fischer, therefore, concluded that sex, class, personality (aggressive/cooperative) and mood (tense/relaxed) of the speaker jointly determined the choice of pronunciation. He added, "In other words, the children were more apt to say 'singing', 'reading', or 'interesting' if they were girls, if their families were above median income, if they had dominating or assertive personalities, and if they were tense—as they might be at the beginning of the interview" (Hickerson, 1980: 90). Other studies however, confirm that the female speakers tend to use more prestigious forms of speech than male speakers of the same social background (Yule, 1996 : 242).

In many cultures, genders are differentiated through speech. In the case of Yana, a native language of California, particular verb endings depend on the sex of the speaker. This amounts to a difference in the grammatical form of the language to match the sex of the speaker. This has been shown also for Koasati speakers, another group of American Indians, studied by Mary Haas (1944). In other languages, as in the case of Island Carib and many related languages of Central and South America, the use of different vocabularies for men and women is not a matter of choice but is prescriptive. This had confused Europeans, who first encountered the Carib Indians in the 16th Century, into thinking that women spoke a different language from men.

Psychologists like Cheris Kramer opine that women are more talkative than men, and female speech is less forceful than that of men. When there is a conversation in a mixed group of men and women, men interrupting women is far greater than the reverse. Women are also reported to use more expressions associated with tentativeness, and use more qualifiers before expressing an opinion (Kramer, 1974).

In English, we find many gender-biased terms and usages, whose bias is predominantly masculine. In English and many other languages, the masculine terms are considered to be grammatically basic, and feminine forms are generally derived from their masculine forms. We may consider, for example, the terms *goddess, lioness, princess* etc. which are derived from *god, lion, prince* respectively. Moreover, masculine terms are frequently used to include women, and the common example is the term *men*. Most recently, however, there has been an attempt to replace with gender-neutral words or phrases, as in the use of *chairperson, mail carrier, fire fighter* etc. in place of the conventional usage of *chairman, mailman, fireman* respectively. There have been attempts also to coin gender-neutral personal and possessive pronouns in the singular that correspond to the plural forms *they, them,* and *their,* which apply to either sex or to both. But it has not become very successful yet, and hence, linguistic sexism still continues.

Ethnic Background and Dialectical Variation

In a multi-ethnic society, it is obvious that different ethnic groups use their variant of the standard dialect, which contains the identifying features of their original language. The case is extremely transparent in the U.S.A., where Afro-Americans have a different social dialect. This is commonly referred to as **Black English**, which is normally considered to be 'bad speech'. One of the distinguishing features of Black English is the frequent absence of the copula (forms of the verb 'to be'), resulting in expressions like *You crazy* or *They mine*. This does not confirm to the rule of Standard English, as the verb *are* is missing in both the cases. Black English is also associated with double negative constructions, as in *I don't know nothing,* which is considered to be illogical.

Multilingualism and Diglossia

It is very commonly assumed that linguistic and cultural boundaries coincide, and hence, people of different cultures tend to speak mutually uintelligible languages. But the common human experience is very different. In most parts of the world, different ethnic group speaking different languages live side by side, and often learn to speak language(s) other than their own mother tongue. This is a typical situation of **multilingualism,** which refers to the use or ability to use two or more languages by the people of a community. The most common form of multilingualism is **bilingualism**, characterized by the ability of a group of people to speak two languages, including their mother tongue. Theoretically speaking, bilingualism refers to the acquisition of complete and equal command over both the languages in question, as is expected from a native speaker. In practice, however, the term is applied more loosely extending to those, who communicate in both the languages.

Bilingualism is common in a multilingual nation like India. This is due to the fact that the States in post-Independent India are organised on language lines. Thus each State is primarily a linguistic State. Each one of them is bounded by other States with different languages. Hence, very commonly, the populations on the border of each of these States speak at least two languages, and are bilinguals. In the State capitals, cities and business centres, where people speaking different languages interact, one may find relatively stable bilingualism, and possibly multilingualism. Canadians speaking French and English, Latinos in the United States of America speaking Spanish and English etc. are the examples of bilingualism. In countries like India, the former Soviet Union, and United States of America, bilingualism is common, because of the history of these nations.

Multilingualism, however, is common in many countries of the world. Let us the take the example of language teaching in India. In a Central School (*Kendriya Vidyalaya*), students are supposed to learn Hindi, English, and the language of the State in which the School is established. If the mother tongue of the student is different from the official State language of his State of domicile, he can speak four languages, including his own mother tongue. A tribal student in India is similarly able to speak four languages : his tribal dialect, the official language of the State of domicile, Hindi, and English. An interesting case of multilingualism may be found among the Native Americans of the northwestern Brazil and the adjoining part of Colombia. This culturally homogeneous area is inhabited by at least twenty different tribes, who are fluent in three, four, or more regional languages. Because of strict tribal exogamy, a child has to learn additional languages of the neighbouring tribes to look for a marital partner during adolescence, thus encouraging multilingualism as a cultural necessity rather than an exception (Salzmann, 1993: 131). Multilingualism, however, is a traditional and asymmetrical phenomenon, as the second and subsequent generation of speakers prefer to acquire the dominant language of the region, thus losing the multilingual character of the group. For example, many Native Americans in the United States of America have achieved near-complete linguistic assimilation, barring only a few elderly members still able to communicate in their native language. The reverse situation is also possible, where there have been attempts to create or revitalise native languages and scripts, as in the case of Santal (Ol Chiki) and Khamti tribes respectively, in India.

In a multilinguistic situation, it is quite possible that different forms of the same language are being used for different purposes. When members of a speech community use two or more varieties of the same language under different conditions and for different functions, Charles A. Ferguson called it as **diglossia**. Ferguson noticed that the "high" variety of the language is associated with education and literacy and used in more formal situations, while the "low" variety is the colloquial one and used for ordinary conversation with relatives and friends. Ferguson cites the examples of the classical and formal Arabic of the Holy Koran, which coexists with diversified and colloquial local forms of Arabic, such as, the Arabic of Baghdad or Cairo or Tunis etc. Similarly, the use of Standard German as the formal variety and the Swiss German in ordinary conversations in Switzerland, the classical and the colloquial Greek in Greece, and so on are the most cited examples of the diglossic varieties in different parts of the world. But in actual speech, it is very difficult to maintain the separability of two different languages or two varieties of the same language by a bilingual. Therefore, more often than not, there is a shift from one to the other during speaking, in other words, **code-switching**.

India presents an excellent example of many diglossic situations. In the State of Bihar, while certain local dialects are used in speaking with elders, a particular subdialect of Western Hindi is used with friends and younger persons. In South India where

Dravidian languages have been spoken for centuries, the Brahman and non-Brahman speech varieties are used by the speakers of different caste affiliations. In North India, high forms of Hindi and Urdu are used on formal occasions and local Hindustani in very informal settings (Khubchandani, 1983). John Gumperz (1964), however, concludes from his survey of speech varieties in Khalapur that villagers use Hindi as the high variety of speech and the local dialect as the low variety. Again, Hindi is divided into high and low, if used in oratorical and conversational styles respectively; while the local Khalapur dialect has its clean (high) and gross (low) varieties, when used with distant acquaintances and elders, and with relatives, children, servants and animals respectively. This fourfold division has been subsequently called **double-nested diglossia** (Fasold, 1984). In India today, despite the spread of education and the impact of popular mass media, dialectical variation is still associated with the castes and caste hierarchy, which poses a real challenge for language planning.

Lingua Franca

In a multilingual area, where people speak divergent languages, there is a strong desire among the groups to arrive at some common agreement in using a common language for the purpose of social or commercial communication. This commonly agreed language of communication is known as **lingua franca**. English is often considered as the lingua franca of the whole world. In the United States of America, English has been the lingua franca for communication between many different speakers of Native American languages. Hindi and Urdu are the lingua francas of India and Pakistan respectively, where people speak many varieties of languages in their own regions. Similarly, although many different tribal languages are spoken in East Africa, Swahili usually serves as the lingua franca, which is spoken in every market place of the region. Hausa is a lingua franca spoken in West Africa, making it easy for communication between the speakers of different tribal dialects. While in some places a lingua franca develops naturally, in some other places it takes shape due to the intervention of the State.

Pidgin and Creole

When the speakers of two or more mutually unintelligible languages develop a need to communicate with each other for some specific purpose, such as trade, **pidgin** often develops. But then, what is the difference between a lingua franca and a pidgin ? While a lingua franca has a broad base of native speakers, pidgin does not have a native speaker of its own. Instead, when two or more groups use their native languages and draw essential elements from them in developing a "marginal language", it is called as a pidgin. Since pidgin serves a limited purpose, it possesses minimum vocabulary and a reduced grammatical structure (it is, however, not devoid of grammar). Therefore, it is much simpler compared to any first language, so as to serve the limited objective of specialised communication. It develops when speakers of different languages have been in regular but limited contact.

A good example of pidgin is **Tok Pisin**, or Melanesian Pidgin English, widely used in Papua New Guinea. It has about 1500 lexical items, 80 per cent of which are derived from English (Fromkin and Rodman, 1978: 268-269). It is known as Neo-Melanesian, and is the lingua franca of about one million people who speak some 700 native languages of Papua New Guinea. It is the first language of about 200,000 households. It has acquired so much prestige that even parliamentary debates are conducted in tok pisin (from talk pidgin) rather than in English (Salzmann, *op. cit.*: 134). The English-based China coast pidgin, the English-based Maori pidgin, Navajo-based pidgin of the American south-west, Congo pidgin in the Congo river basin are some other examples of pidgins developed mostly as a consequence of European colonialism and expansion of trade in different parts of the world.

Pidgin develops suddenly as the need arises and disappears easily when it is no longer in use. Therefore, it is a transitory product along with the course of history. The history of Vietnam is a good case is point. When Vietnam was ruled by the French as a part of French Indochina, a French-based pidgin came into use. But after the defeat of the French in 1954 and the subsequent evacuation of French defence forces, the pidgin became extinct. With the coming of the United States of America's combat forces in 1960, an English-based pidgin developed to cater for the need, which again became obsolete after the withdrawal of the U.S. forces in 1973.

Although pidgin is simple with fewer items of vocabulary to cater to the immediate need of the communicating groups, it has a structure of its own and is readily adaptable to changing circumstances. The reduction or elimination of inflectional affixes, the use of morphemic repetition for intensification, and simplified syntactic constructions etc. lead some scholars to claim that pidgins in geographically different places display a remarkable degree of structural consistency (Salzmann, *op. cit.*: 133-134).

It is asserted above that no pidgin has a native speaker. But under some pressing circumstances, the pidgin may be adopted by a speech community as its native or first language, when it is called as a **creole**. Since a creole needs to be a fully developed language with more lexical items and broad rules of grammar than a pidgin, the latter is said to be **creolised**. This may be considered as an opposite process to **pidginisation**, which has been discussed above. The Haitian French-based creole, the English spoken in some parts of Jamaica, Gullah—an English-based creole spoken by the descendants of the African slaves on the islands off the coast of Georgia and South Carolina, Louisiana spoken by the whites and blacks in Louisiana, Krio spoken by the Sierra Leoneans etc. are good examples of creoles. For historical reasons, pidgins and creoles are found in coastal areas of the equatorial belt, where speakers belonging to diverse languages have had to meet and communicate among each other for the purpose of territorial and trade expansion.

In more recent times, there has been a process of **decreolisation** in operation where creoles have evolved. This is because, with the spread of education, greater social prestige has been attached to the standard language, from which the creole had been derived. This has resulted in the tendency to use fewer forms and structures of creole than the standard language. But since the use of the language ultimately depends on the speaker, one may find three possible varieties in these situations. It may be a **basilect**, closer to the basic variety, or an **acrolect** with more features of the external model. Sometimes one may encounter a **mesolect,** which represents a range of different varieties, some with many and some with few creole features. This range of varieties, which evolve after the creoles have been created, is known as the **post-creole continuum** (Yule, 1996: 235).

7

DIRECTIONS OF LANGUAGE CHANGE

Languages are subject to change like cultures, and hence, no language is static or unchanging. The English language has undergone extensive change between the old and the modern English periods. If we look at the linguistic history of England, we come across different languages and their mixtures being spoken in England over many years. England was first invaded by the Romans in the 1st Century A.D. and became a Roman colony. With the collapse of the Romans empire, the Germanic-speaking tribes began invading England in the 5th Century A.D. from the North-western Europe, including Saxons, Angles, and Frisians, among others. The invaders had to fight with the Celtic-speaking inhabitants of England. The Celtic tribes of England, who spoke Scottish, were confined to the North of England, and the remaining Celtic speakers were pushed into Wales and Cornwall. Of all the pre-English languages once spoken in England, only Welsh has survived the test of time, and is still spoken in north and central Wales. The original Celtic language of Scotland became extinct. When Gaelic speakers from Ireland moved into Scotland in the 15th Century, a synthetic language, Scots-Gaelic developed in that region, which is still spoken by a minority of the population. Irish Gaelic, however, is still spoken in Ireland, but by a small minority of the inhabitants.

During the period from the 5th Century A.D. until the 11th Century, which linguists distinguish as the period of Old English, the Germanic-speaking invaders contributed immensely to the development of the English language. The most basic terms of English, therefore, had a Germanic origin. Some English words and their Germanic roots are given below:

English Word	*Its Germanic Root*
Man	Mann
Woman	Wif
Child	Cild
House	Hus
Eat	Etan
Drink	Drincan

During the 8th and 9th centuries, however, the Anglo-Saxons, as they were called because of their original tribal names, began to convert to Christianity from paganism. Since the religious language of Christianity was then Latin, the English language incorporated many Latin words in its vocabulary. The words, *Bishop, Candle, Church, Priest, School,* etc. in Modern English are derived from Latin, either directly or indirectly.

The English language was not only influenced by the languages of the Germanic speaking invaders of England, but also by other languages spoken by subsequent invaders. It has borrowed considerably from the Scandinavian languages because the north-eastern part of England was ruled by the Vikings from the 8th to 10th centuries. The Vikings were the speakers of Old Norse, a Scandinavian language. Modern English words like, *give, law, leg, skin, sky, skirt, they* etc., are derived from Old Norse.

When the Normans conquered England in 1066 A.D., it marked the beginning of the period of Middle English, which continued until the 15th Century A.D. The French speaking Normans took over all of England, and much of Scotland and Wales. French became the court language and language of the nobility of England for a considerable period during the Norman rule, although the language of the rural peasantry remained English. Nevertheless, modern English words like *defence, army, court, prison, tax, mutton* etc. and many nasalised sounds were rooted in French, which were uncommon in old English.

Linguists consider that modern English had its beginning in the 15th century and countinues till the present time. Although middle English was not drastically different from modern English, compared with old English, it was different to hear, because of different vowel sounds. This may be made clear with an excerpt from the writings of Chaucer in the late 14th century in his, *The Canterbury Tales:*

> "She was cleped Madame Eglentyne
> Ful wel she song the service dyvyne,
> Entuned in hir nose ful semely,
> And Frenshe she spak ful faire and fetisly."

Between 1400 and 1600, the period that separated Chaucer and Shakespeare, the English language underwent many changes to gradually reach its present form. The change in the language is reflected in its structural components, such as, **phonology**, **morphology** and **syntax**, as well as the changes in the **vocabulary**. All these four components went through the process of either **addition** or **loss** or **change** to have evolved in their new forms.

PHONOLOGICAL CHANGE

One of the most significant sound changes between middle and modern English is the quality of the **vowel sounds**. Although the general form of some words has remained the same, their vowel sounds changed considerably. We shall see in the following examples the lengthening of the vowel sounds in modern English, compared to the earlier ones

Earlier English	*Modern English*
mi:s	*mays* (mice)
hu:s	*haws* (house)
ge:s	*gi:s* (geese)
spo:n	*spu:n* (spoon)
brɛ:ken	*bre:k* (break)

This process of change in vowel sounds in English started around the time of the death of Chaucer in 1400 A.D. and was still taking place when Shakespeare died in 1616 A.D., and is commonly known as **the great vowel shift** in the English language.

Between the times of Chaucer and Shakespeare, another phonological change occurred in English with the loss of /x/ sound in some words, which is evident in the following examples

Middle English	*Modern English*
nixt	*night*
druxt	*drought*
saux	*saw*

In some cases, however, instead of being silent, the /x/ sound was pronounced as /f/, as in the words, *rough* and *tough* etc. In some other cases, it was vocalised to become a vowel, as in *hollow* and *sorrow* from */holx/* and */sorx/* respectively. But the /x/ sound has been retained in Scottish in some of these words.

There is another significant change from middle to new English, which involves a reversal in position of two adjoining sounds. This change is referred to as **metathesis** and can be found in the following examples:

Middle English	*Modern English*
bridd	*bird*
frist	*first*
hros	*horse*
acsian	*ask*

Sometimes we come across instances of sound change in the form of an addition of a new sound to the middle of a word. This change is known as **epenthesis**, and is exemplified in the following pairs of words :

aemtig - empty, spinel - spindle, timr - timber etc.

Sound change involving the addition of a sound at the beginning of a word is known as **prothesis** and may be found in some languages other than English. It is very common in the change of pronunciation of some words from Latin to Spanish, as found in the following examples:

schola - escuela (school)
spiritus - espiritu (spirit)

This is the reason why Spanish speakers initially pronounce *estrange* and *estory* to *strange* and *story* respectively, when they begin to learn English as their second language.

MORPHOLOGICAL CHANGE

Between the middle and modern English period, there have been some changes in the rules of morphology, parallel to the phonological changes. One of the remarkable changes in the morphological rules is the **addition** of *-able*. Originally many French words with *-able* were borrowed by English, which eventually was made applicable even to many words of Germanic origin, such as, *doable* and *washable* with Germanic roots *do* and *wash* respectively.

The **loss** of morphological rule could be observed in the causative verb formation rules of middle and modern English. In middle English, the causative verb was formed with adding a suffix /-yan/ to the adjective. Subsequently, we find this rule in the form of an addition of a suffix *-en* (instead of -yan) to the adjective, as in the case of *sweeten, redden* etc. This rule is no more in use in modern English, and we do not hear of causative verbs like *green-en, blue-en* and similar other forms.

Change in the morphological rule between the periods of the middle and modern English can be seen in the case of addition of /-ing/ to nouns, as has been done in modern English with the verbs. It is common that the present continuous forms of verbs like go + ing (going) or sleep + ing (sleeping) in modern English add /-ing/ to the present indefinite forms of verbs. But in middle English, there were many nouns with the addition of /-ing/, such as, *viking* from the noun *wic* or 'bay'. In modern English, we only find very limited instances of such forms with a suffix of /-ing/ to the nouns, such as, *roofing, flooring* etc. It shows a restricted application of this phonological rule in modern English, compared to its old form, and hence, there are not many nouns with the suffix of /-ing/, referring to the material used for something.

SYNTACTIC CHANGE

The syntactic rules pertaining to the **negative construction** underwent some changes from middle to modern English. In modern English, negation is expressed with the addition of *not* or *do not* or *never* or *no*. These usages are clear from the following examples:

(a) I am *not* playing
(b) I *do not* play.

(c) I *never* play.
(d) I deserve *no* reward.

In middle English, however, the negation was expressed by *ne*, which occurred before the auxiliary verb or before the main verb, in the absence of an auxiliary verb in the sentence. The following example provided by Fromkin and Rodman (1978: 302) in this context is worth analysing:

paet he *na* sippan geboren *ne* wurde
(that he never after born not would be)
that he should be never be born after that

Two remarkable differences between middle and modern English can be noticed from the above example. One can easily notice the difference in the **word order.** But what is more interesting is the use of **double negatives** (*na* and *ne*), which some grammarians consider as ungrammatical. Moreover, in old English the negative expression came up at the beginning, as it preceded the auxiliary verb. But in modern English, with the changing word order, *not* usually comes after the auxiliary, as we use them in contracted forms like *can't, won't, haven't, wasn't* etc.

Another dimension of change between middle and modern English can be noticed in the rules formulating **negative constructions.** In middle English, mere addition of *not* at the end of an affirmative sentence could change it to negative, as in the following:

(a) I deny it *not*.
(b) I love thee *not*, therefore pursue me *not*.

But in modern English, *not* has to precede the main verb of the clause, and a *do* in its proper tense must be used, as in the following examples:

(a) I *do not* deny it.
(b) I *do not* love you, therefore, *don't* pursue me.

There is another change of syntactic rule from middle to modern English, which is associated with the rules of **comparative** and **superlative** constructions. In modern English the addition of *-er* or the insertion of *more* denote comparative formulation, and the addition of *-est* or the insertion of *most* to the adjective denote superlative construction. But in old English, it was perfectly grammatical to use double comparatives or double superlatives as in the cases of *more lower, most shamefullest* and the like.

SEMANTIC CHANGES

Semantic changes in any language may be effected when the language gains or loses semantic items. Sometimes, particular lexical items stand for a different meaning, for which language also changes. There are, however, three ways in which a lexical item may change semantically, such as, broadening, narrowing down or shifting of meaning, which we shall discuss below.

Sometimes the meaning of a given word becomes **broader,** encompassing many words of the same "semantic field". For example, the word *holiday* originally meant holy day or a day of religious significance. But in the course of time, it got associated with a day without work. Similarly, the word *picture* was used for 'painted representations', which gradually broadened in meaning to even include a picture with a camera. The word *bird* originally meant 'young birds', but eventually was used for all birds.

The reverse process of broadening is the process of **narrowing down** of meaning. In the 17th Century English, the word *meat* referred to the food of any kind, and what today we understand by meat was called *flesh.* This shows the process of narrowing down of meaning with respect to certain words. Similarly, the word *deer* originally meant an animal or a beast in general, which has been narrowed down today to refer to a particular kind of animal. Once upon a time, *liquor* was synonymous with any kind of liquid, and more strangely, the word *girl* meant a young person of either sex, which have undergone the process of narrowing down of meaning with the passage of time.

The **shift** in meaning of a lexical item is also a manifestation of linguistic change, which is present in abundance in the English language. In middle English, *lust* simply meant pleasure and did not have a sexual overtone as in the modern English. Similarly, *immoral* represented something uncustomary and did not have anything to do with morality as it is understood now. In old English, *silly* meant happy; its meaning shifted during the middle English period to naive, and is used today to mean foolish.

The shift in meaning in a language is not only restricted to individual lexical items, but extends sometimes to changes effected in an entire **semantic field**. If any one of the lexical items of a semantic field assumes a metaphorical use, other items in the same semantic field automatically undergo parallel semantic changes. For example, when *goose* was metaphorically used for foolishness, the same meaning was extended to words like *cuckoo, pigeon, coot* and *turkey*. Similarly, among the antonyms *hot* and *cold*, when *hot* is metaphorically used in a phrase like *hot news* (referring to the news that is just breaking), almost automatically *cold news* is understood as the opposite, meaning news that has become stale.

LEXICAL CHANGES

In a language like English, the vocabulary or the lexicon is enriched mostly by the process of adding new items from within the language and from outside. However, the language has lost some of its words, which is though much less, compared to the new items being added to the language. Addition to the English lexicon has been effected by various means, and we shall discuss some of them below.

One process of adding to the number of lexical items is **compounding,** or recombining old words to form new ones, with new meanings. Thousands of new words have entered into English in this way. There has been a blending of two root words to give a new meaning, which may not be drastically different from their respective meanings. For example, *servantmaid, icecap, afternoon, chickenhearted, bigmouth, moreover, takeover, undergo, water-cooler* and many such words have been created through this process of compounding. The words *ethnosemantics, ethnobiology* etc. that we frequently use in anthropology have also evolved through this process.

Similar to the process of compounding is the process of **blending** through which words are also recombined to give new meanings. Although very often confused, the process of blending is less than compounding, as the original root words are not exactly retained in the new word, as in the case of compounding. Take for example, *smog*, which is formed by the blending of *smoke* and *fog*. Similarly, blending of *motor* and *hotel* gives rise to *motel*, where the new word loses some parts of the original words. In an exactly similar fashion, blending of *urine* and *analysis* has resulted in *urinalysis*, which has attained full lexical status in English like the previous examples that have been discussed above. There are, however, still certain words in English, which are formed by the process of blending, and have limited acceptance in the language. One example of this kind of word is *broasted*, formed by the blending of *broiled* and *roasted*.

Most often **acronyms,** which are derived from the initials of several words, are pronounced as they are spelt, and are recognised as new words in the language. Words like *VCR* (Video Cassette Recorder), *CD* (Compact Discs), *UNESCO* (United Nations Educational Social and Cultural Organisation), *NATO* (North Atlantic Treaty Organisation), *RADAR* (Radio Detecting and Ranging), *ATM* (Automatic Teller Machine), *PIN* (Personal Identification Number or Postal Index Number) etc. are pronounced as single words and are examples of English acronyms.

Sometimes a new word is coined or created to fit some purpose, which is known as **word coinage,** and is another process of lexical addition to the language. *Kodak, Nylon, Orlon* etc., the names for some consumer items, and specific brand names like *Xerox, Brillo, Vaseline, Kleenex* etc. are often used as general names for many brands of the product.

New words are also being formed in English by deleting the affix of the old words. This process is known as **back-formation.** This process can be seen in words like *hawk, swindle, peddle* and *edit* etc. that have come into being from the original words *hawker, swindler, peddler* and *editor* respectively.

In English language we come across many words, which are **abbreviations** of the original longer words, but are subsequently recognised as adequately meaning the whole words, and are added up to the vocabulary. Some of these abbreviated forms are: *bike, math, gym, phone, ad, doc* etc. which are well understood by the English speakers.

Borrowing is another process that effects lexical change. This is the process in which a language or a dialect incorporates some lexical elements from another language or dialect directly or through an intermediary language or dialect. In English, about three-fifths of its nearly 20,000 words are borrowed from other languages. We have earlier discussed Germanic, Scandinavian and French elements in English vocabulary and the historical reasons behind their incorporation. The English words *drama, comedy, tragedy, physics,* and *zoology* have come from Greek, and the Greek root can be noticed in the words *acrophobia* and *thermometer.* Latin has contributed many words to English, such as, *exit, scientific, advantage, bonus, quorum,* and *describe.* From Dutch, words like *freight, leak, pump* and *yacht* have been borrowed. Many musical terms have been borrowed from Italian, such as, *opera, piano,* and *balcony.* Some English words have been borrowed from Arabic, like, *alcohol, algebra,* and *zero.* Some of the words of everyday use have been borrowed from Spanish, including *barbecue, cockroach, guitar,* and *ranch.* Even some Hindi words like *raj, rajah, maharaja,* and *bandobust* have found a place in the English language.

Lexical change in English is also due to the loss of some of its words, although the magnitude of loss is almost nothing compared to the borrowing. The loss of words from the old English is evidenced when one reads the old classics. For example, *beseem* (suitable), *mammet* (doll or puppet), *wherefore* (why) and many such words are no longer in use now, causing loss to the language.

Like English, all other languages undergo change, and its study has kept many linguists busy understanding the historical and genetic relationship between different languages of the world. From the study of linguistic change one gets the feeling that change is an inevitable process in a language, as in a culture. Further, all languages are rule-governed, and hence, there are corresponding changes in the grammatical rules of the language over a period of time, as we have seen the changes between old and modern English.

8

LANGUAGE FAMILIES IN THE WORLD

For many historical reasons, we find today, that some languages are spoken much more widely than others. During the post-mediaeval period, when expansion and colonisation was at its peak, the process of diffusion of languages from Europe to Asia, America and the Pacific continued as a supplementary to the expansionist venture. This resulted in the breaking up of communication barrier, which made the world to look linguistically closer and simpler. But, if we look at the different parts of the world at around 1500 A.D., we find that each major geographical region with a natural boundary was represented by a major language, although many local dialects were spoken within the region. Around this time, the whole world area could be divided into five major regions, such as, Eurasia, Africa, North America, South America, and Oceania, within which groups of closely related languages were spoken. It was also common that in these regions, some isolated or unconnected languages were spoken, indicating either migration or forcible displacement of the speakers of some languages to the fringe of the region, where the language survived further onslaught. In any case, it is interesting to know the distribution of languages and language groups in different parts of the world, and their genetic connections, which might throw some light on the history of possible connections between different population groups. Tracing relationships between languages might help supplement knowledge of the historical origin and movement of peoples, which could be of great significance to a culture historian or an archaeologist.

It must be, however, made clear at this point that linguistic affiliation is only one kind of historical evidence used in tracing the origin and diffusion of cultures. This is because of the fact that populations may adopt a new language without changing their cultural identity; or conversely, culture change might take place without corresponding linguistic change. Similarly, speakers of an isolated language might not be taken for the direct descendants of an ancient group of population, without other hard evidences. But it is commonly experienced that the dominant language of a region takes precedence over others, and sometimes it replaces the local dialects, as we have seen Latin replacing many southern Furopean languages.

In order to study the relationship between different languages, linguists often use terminologies that have their origin in biology. For example, **language family** refers to a group of languages of common origin, which is proved by close comparison and reconstruction of the **protolanguage,** from which all of them have evolved. **Language phylum,** on the other hand, refers to a group of languages that might have a common origin, which has not been established very firmly as in the case of a language family. Sometimes, a group of languages are traditionally bound together, mostly as languages being spoken for ages in a geographical area, rather than claiming a strong relationship among themselves is known as a **language group**. On the contrary, the languages or language families that show no affiliation whatsoever to other languages of the region are called **language isolates.** In most cases, it is assumed that language isolates represent the population that preceded the spread of a dominant language family or phylum into the region.

LANGUAGES OF EURASIA

Now if we look at **Eurasia,** we find the following language families, phyla, groups and isolates being spoken:

I. Indo-European

Indo-European is the **largest** single family in the world in its geographical expansion and the number of its speakers. Its speakers stretch from Western Europe to the Indian sub-continent. Although it has many extinct languages that are known through inscriptions and early written sources, it is divided into the following eight modern branches according to their geographical distribution.

Indo-Iranian: This branch is further divided into *Indic* and *Iranian* divisions. The Indic division includes Sanskrit and the modern languages spoken in India, Pakistan and Sri Lanka, such as, Hindi, Bengali, Punjabi, Urdu, Sinhalese etc., including Romany, the language used by the Gypsies throughout the world. The Iranian division includes several dialects of modern Persian, including Pashto (Afghani) and Kurdish.

Balto-Slavic: This has again two divisions; *Baltic* includes Lithuanian, Latvian and the extinct Prussian languages. *Slavic* constitutes a large group spoken in central and eastern Europe, including Russian, Ukrainian, Polish, Czech, Slovak, Serbo-Croatian, Bulgarian etc.

Germanic: This branch includes the languages spoken in northern and western Europe, including the British Isles, and the languages spoken are: English, German, Dutch, Flemish, Swedish, Danish, Norwegian and Icelandic.

Italic: These are the languages that are the descendants of Latin and closely related dialects spoken in Italy at the time of the Roman Empire, such as, Portuguese, Spanish, French, Italian, Romanian etc.

Celtic: Although once spoken over western Europe and the British Isles, Celtic is today confined to the speakers of Irish, Scots Gaelic, Welsh and Breton (in northern France).

Hellenic (Greek), *Albanian*, and *Armenian* consist of a single modern language each.

II. Ural-Altaic

The Ural-Altaic phylum is divided into *Uralic* family and *Altaic* division, which is further divided into three languages families. It is spread over a large area with few natural boundaries, which is reflected in the intersecting and overlapping of various languages. Significantly, most of its speakers are/or were pastoral nomads, and their frequent mobility might have contributed to the distribution of the languages.

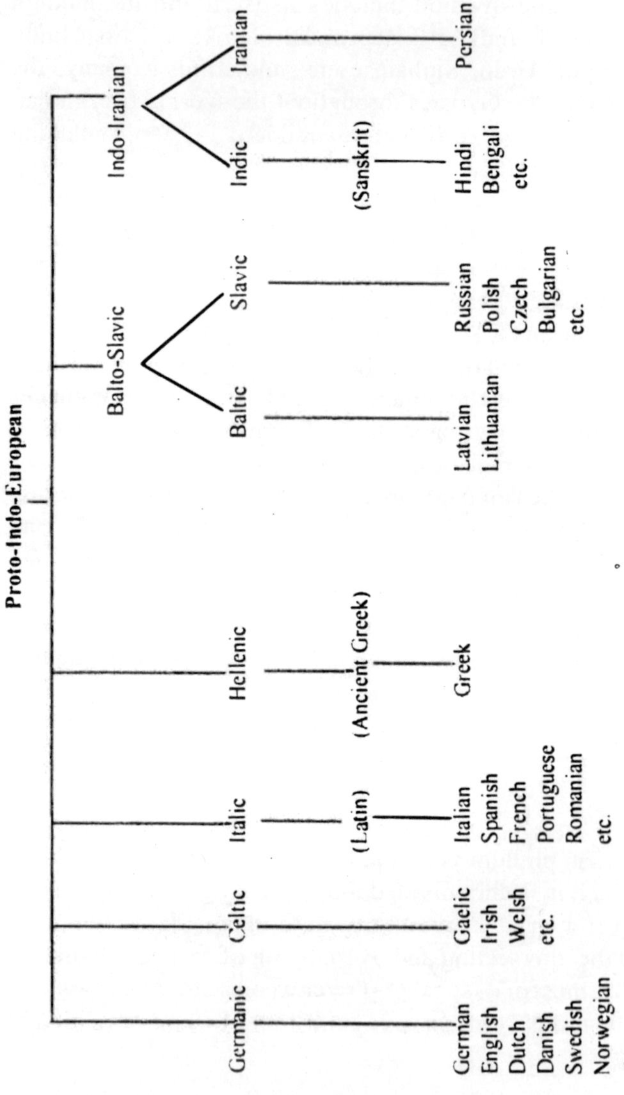

Fig. 8.1: Family Tree of Proto-Indo-European

Uralic: This family is also known as *Finno-Ugric,* which includes Hungarian, Finnish, several small languages spoken along the Volga in Russia (like, Cheremis and Mordwin etc.), and some languages of central Siberia.

Altaic: This is made of three language families, such as, (a) *Turkic,* consisting Turkish and closely related languages like Tatar and Kirghiz of southern Siberia and central Asia, and Yakut in northern Siberia; (b) *Mongol,* a family of closely related languages in Mongolia; and (c) *Manchu-Tungus,* spoken in much of Manchuria and Siberia.

III. Sino-Tibetan

The Sino-Tibetan phylum consists of three language families. (a) *Tibeto-Burman* includes Tibetan and many languages spoken in the Malayan Peninsula, such as, Lolo, Kachin, Garo etc.; (b) *Chinese* is a family of Mandarin of northern China, Cantonese of southern China, and other minor languages like Wu, Hakka and Min; (c) *Tai* includes Thai or Siamese, Lao, and many other languages spoken in China and Indo-China, such as, Miao, Yao, Shan, Kadai etc. This family is of disputed status, whether being a family in itself or a part of Austroasiatic phylum. The proponents of the latter theory suggest that similarities between Tai and Chinese have nothing to do with common origin, but are due to borrowing only.

IV. Dravidian

Dravidian is spoken by a large number of populations in the Indian subcontinent. Four south Indian languages, such as, Telugu, Tamil, Kannada and Malayalam belong to this family. In Baluchistan, Brahui is a part of this family. The Tamil speakers of Sri Lanka also speak Dravidian. It is hypothesised that the Indian sub-continent had a majority of original Dravidian speakers who were pushed into the south by the invading speakers of Indo-European language.

V. Caucasian

This group of languages are those spoken in the mountainous areas of the former Soviet Union, between the Black and Caspian seas.

Many of these languages do not belong to one language family, despite having some common characteristics. The representatives of this group are: Georgian, Azerbaijani, Abkhazian, Kabardian, Ubykh etc.

VI. Japanese-Korean

This phylum consists of two languages, Japanese and Korean, which in the past were considered to be isolated languages. However, both these languages have an ancient genetic relationship. There is even a suggestion that this phylum has a remote connection with the Ural-Altaic phylum.

VII. Paleo-Siberian

This group consists of Yeneseian and Luorawetlan, two small language families, and two language isolates, Yukaghir and Gilyak. The speakers live in northeastern Siberia, and primarily depend upon hunting, fishing and reindeer herding.

VIII. Austroasiatic

The Austroasiatic phylum consists of three widely dispersed language families; (a) *Munda* is spoken by many small tribal communities in eastern India; (b) *Mon-Khmer* has speakers in the countries of Burma, Cambodia and Vietnam; and (c) *Nicobarese,* spoken by a small island population in the Bay of Bengal.

IX. Basque

It is a language isolate located in western France and northeastern Spain, and is remotely related to the languages of the Caucasian group.

X. Ainu

Ainu is again a language isolate of northern Japan, and its speakers are identified with an ancient pre-Japanese culture. Some linguists are of the view that Ainu has some similarities with several American Indian languages.

XI. Andamanese

Andamans is a group of islands in the Bay of Bengal, and the native speakers there use Andamanese, which is a language isolate. Although it is different from the neighbouring languages of the region, because of physical isolation of the Andaman population, some people believe it has a remote connection with the Papuan languages of New Guinea.

LANGUAGES OF AFRICA

In **Africa** and the adjoining parts of Asia, we find three major language families and two language phyla being spoken, a brief sketch of which is given below:

I. Afroasiatic

Four out of the total of five language families under this language phylum constitute the major languages being spoken in different parts of Africa. Various families of Afroasiatic language are: (a) *Semitic,* which has again two divisions. The northern division consists of Hebrew, Aramaic, and extinct languages like, Phoenician and Akkadian. The southern division consists of Arabic, spoken widely in the middle-east, and Amharic, the main language of Ethiopia; (b) *Egyptian,* which is now extinct, surviving only as a liturgical language used by Coptic Christians; (c) *Berber,* which is spoken by the dispersed populations in northern Africa; (d) *Cushitic,* spoken in east Africa, includes Somali, Galla, Beja etc.; and (e) *Chadic,* which is spoken in west-central Africa, around lake Chad, Hausa being the largest language in the family.

II. Congo-Kordofanian

This phylum has two divisions: the first being *Kordofanian,* a small group of languages, spoken in the Sudan in Nilo-Saharan area. The second division, *Niger-Congo* consists of a large number of languages spoken in the African continent south of Sahara, and is divided into the following six groups; (a) *West Atlantic* that includes Wolof, Fulani and other languages of Senegal, Guinea and

Gambia; (b) *Mande* which includes Mande, Kpellé, Malinke, and other languages of the Ivory Coast; (c) *Gur* spoken in Nigeria and neighbouring countries that includes languages like Tallensi and Nupe; (d) *Kwa* consists of Akan, Kru, Ewe, Yoruba, Ibo etc. and spoken in Liberia and Nigeria; (e) *Adamawe-Eastern*, a scattered group of languages spoken in the area east of Lake Chad; and (f) *Benue-Congo*, which is spoken in Nigeria and includes the Bantu group of languages spread throughout the Congo, and eastern and southeastern parts of Africa. Bantu, in fact, consists of a dozen of barely differentiated languages, including Ganda, Kongo, Kikuyu, Rawanda, Swazi, Zulu, Swahili etc.

III. Nilo-Saharan

This family has three branches, such as, (a) *Songhai*, spoken in Mali, in the area along the river Niger; (b) *Saharan*, a large group of languages spoken in the east of Lake Chad; and (c) *Sudanic*, located north of Lake Victoria, and includes Nubian and Nilotic languages (like, Nuer and Masai).

IV. Khoisan

This family consists of many languages spoken in the arid regions of South Africa, and includes the languages of Bushmen and Hottentot. These, in turn, are subdivided into many languages and dialects, which are significantly associated with many groups of hunters in the region. However, Khoisan languages are also spoken in isolated pockets, further to the north in Tanzania.

V. Austronesian

The languages spoken in Madagascar belong to the Austronesian family of languages, which is spoken largely is the Pacific.

LANGUAGES IN OCEANIA

When we turn our attention to **Oceania,** we find again a large group of languages spoken, which could be categorised into various phyla, families and isolates. These include many ancient languages of Australia and Southeast Asia and their different variations spoken in the groups of islands and archipelagoes in the Pacific

I. Austronesian

The Austronesian family is the most widespread family of languages, as it is spoken from Madagascar of the east coast of Africa to Ha'waii through the archipelagoes of Southeast Asia. It consists of about 500 languages. It can be divided into two divisions of language groups: (a) the *Western* division has many languages including Malay, Indonesian, Javanese, Tagalog, Ilocano and other languages of the Philippines; the aboriginal language of Taiwan; the tribal languages of Vietnam and Cambodia; Malagasy and other languages of Madagascar; and languages spoken in several islands of Micronesia and New Guinea; (b) the *Eastern* division consists of languages of Melanesian branch spoken in Fiji, New Caledonia, New Hebrides, parts of Solomon archipelago, northern and eastern coastal parts of New Guinea. The Micronesian branch consists of Gilbertese, Ponapean, and other languages of Micronesia. The Polynesian branch consists of Gilbertese, Ponapean, and other languages of Micronesia. The Polynesian branch, however, includes Maori, Hawaiian, Marquesan, Tongan, and Samoan languages.

II. Australian

The Australian phylum consists of more than 200 different languages spoken by the aboriginal population of Australia. It includes the northern languages of Tiwi, Murngin, Yir Yoront etc., and Kariera and Arunta of south, central, and western desert areas. All these languages appear to be genetically related, and may be put into one language family.

III. Papuan

This may well be categorised as a macrophylum that consists of a large number of languages, which might be genetically related. It includes several hundred languages of the interior, southern and western New Guinea, some languages spoken on the eastern Indonesian islands of Halmahera, Timor and Alor, in New Britain, and in parts of the Solomon islands in Melanesia.

IV. Tasmanian

Tasmanian is primarily considered to be a language isolate, as its relationship with other languages has not been verified.

LANGUAGES OF NORTH AMERICA

The whole of America contains a rich responsitory of languages like the other continents of the world. But **North America,** which stretches from Greenland down to Mexico, is relatively well re-searched, and our knowledge of north American languages is far better than other regions of the world. The languages spoken in north America are numerous, and may be divided into macrophyla, phyla, families, and unaffiliated families and isolates. The major divisions of the north American languages are discussed below:

I. Macro-Algonkian

This phylum consists of two large group of related languages, which are further sub-divided into language families and language isolates. One of the largest families included under the phylum is *Algonkian*, which includes languages like Ojibwa, Naskapi and Cree in eastern Canada; Micmac, Penobscot, Delaware, and Powhatan along the eastern seaboard; Shawnee, Menomini, Fox, and Kickpoo in the Ohio valley and Great Lake area; Arapaho, Blackfoot, and Cheyenne in the northern Great Plains; and Wiyot and Yurok in California, which are sometimes classified together as *Ritwan*.

Another large family of *Muskogean* and other smaller languages constitute the second division of the phylum. Muskogean is mostly spoken in the southeastern part of the continent, and includes Creek, Koasati, Choctaw-Chickasaw languages.

II. Aztec-Tanoan

This phylum consists of two language families, such as, *Uto-Aztecan* and *Kiowa-Tanoan*. The centre of the Uto-Aztecan family is in the Great Basin and Colorado valley, but is distributed up to central Mexico. Major languages under this family include Ute and Paiute in the Great Basin; Shoshone and Comanche in the Great

Plains; Hopi, Pima and Papago in the southwestern United States; Luiseno and Gabrileno tribal languages in California; Cora, Yaqui and Tarahumara in northern Mexico; and Nahuatl, the language of the Aztecs in central Mexico. Kiowa from the Kiowa-Tanoan family is a Plains language, and Tanoan is a small group of eastern Pueblo languages being spoken by Jemez, Taos, Isleta, San Juan and so on.

III. Macro-Siouan

This phylum consists of three language families and two isolates. The *Iroquoian* family consists of Huron, Iroquois, and other minor languages in eastern Canada and New York, and Cherokee and Tuscarora in the Carolinas. The *Siouan* family is represented by Dakota, Omaha, Osage, Crow and Mandan languages in the Plains, and by Biloxi, Tutelo and Ofo in the southeast. The *Caddon* family is located mainly in the southern Plains and is represented by Caddo, Wichita and Pawnee languages. The phylum also includes *Catawba* and *Yuchi* language isolates.

IV. Hokan

The Hokan phylum includes the much diversified *Yuman* family of languages and a few language isolates that are scattered from California to Central America. The Yuman family is located in southern California and along the river Colorado. It includes languages like, Yuma, Mohave and Havasupai. It also includes Pomo, Karok, Yana and Achumawi-Atsugewi in California, Seri in Sonora, Coahuiltecan in northeast Mexico, Tlapanecan and Tequistlatecan in southern Mexico, and Jicaque in Honduras.

V. Penutian

This phylum is represented by many diverse languages and language isolates of north and central America. This includes Tsimshian in coastal British Columbia; Chinookan, Sahaptian and Nez Perce in Oregon and northern California; and Wintun, Miwok and Yokuts in central California. It is also believed that the Mayan family in Mexico is affiliated with Penutian language phylum.

VI. Na-Dene

This phylum includes the *Athabascan* family, spread over a wide area in north America. The family covers most of western Canada represented by Chipewayan, Dogrib, Sarsi and Chilcotin languages; northern California and Oregon; Arizona; New Mexico; and neighbouring areas of the southwest, where it includes Navaho and the Lipan, Mescalero and other groups of Apache languages. Other divisions of the phylum are distributed from the north to the south coast of Alaska and British Columbia, and are represented by Eyak, Tlingit and Haida languages.

VII. Oto-Manguean

Languages of this phylum are confined to the mountainous region in middle America, which include *Zapotecan, Mixtecan, Popolocan, Manguean* and *Chinantecan* language families.

VIII. Eskimo-Aleut

This language family has two branches, as is clear from the name of the family. The Eskimo branch is spoken in the vast stretch of area from Point Barrow in the northern Alaska to the eastern Greenland without much of differentiation. However, it is highly diversified in the region of western Alaska. Aleut is spoken in southern Alaska and the Aleutian islands.

IX. Wakashan

This family consists of several languages spoken in the northwest of North America, and includes Nootka, Kwakiutl and Heiltsuk languages. Related families to Wakashan include Salish and Chimakuan language families in the western U.S. and Canada, and Kutenai, a language isolate in the eastern plateau region of the United States. Because of their similarities, Edward Sapir had proposed that these three small language families and Kutenai should be combined with Algonkian to constitute an Algonkian-Wakasha phylum.

X. Tarascan

This is a language isolate of Michoacan in Mexico with a few thousand speakers, who had once successfully resisted the Aztec empire.

Besides these phyla, families and language isolates, there are still some **unaffiliated** families and isolates in north America, including the Yuki family of northern California; the Keresan language isolate distributed in several Pueblo communities; and two extinct language isolates, Karankawa on the Texas coast and Timucua of southern Florida.

LANGUAGES OF SOUTH AMERICA

Following Greenberg's regrouping, the languages spoken in **South America** are divided into three macrophyla, as presented below:

I. Macro-Chibchan

This macrophylum has three main divisions: (a) The *Chibchan* family has its centre in Colombia and extends into central and south America. It includes Chibcha, Andaqui, Tunebo etc. in Colombia; Cuna in Panama; and Rama in Nicaragua. (b) The *Waican* languages spoken by the Yanomamo and other people along the Venezuelan-Brazilian border. (c) Diverse languages spoken in the northern and western parts of the continent, including Waro and Yaruro in Venezuela; Esmerelda in Ecuador; and Yunca in Peru.

II. Ge-Pano-Carib

This is an unusually large macrophylum with the following major divisions; (a) *Macro-Ge* phylum, which includes *Ge*, a compact family of languages spoken in central Brazil. (b) *Macro-Panoan* phylum spoken in Brazil, Paraguay, Bolivia, and Peru. (c) *Macro-Carib* phylum including the Carib family spoken in northeastern Brazil, Venezuela and the Guyanas. Other families include Witoto, Huarpe in Argentina, Nambicuara in south-central Brazil, and Bororo in Brazil and eastern Bolivia.

III. Andean-Equatorial

This is also a large macrophylum, consisting of (a) the *Arawakan* family spoken in Venezuela, the Guyanas, Brazil and the West Indies; (b) the *Tupi-Guarani* family distributed in the Amazon basin in central Brazil, southeastern Brazil, and Paraguay; (c) the *Quechumaran* phylum spoken in Peru, Bolivia and Argentina; (d) the *Jivaro* division including Jivaro, Yaruro and other language isolates of northern Peru and Ecuador; (e) the *Tucanoan* division spoken in northwestern Brazil and Colombia; and (f) the *Chon* group of languages, including Ona, Yahgan, and Araucanian which are highly diversified and are considered as language isolates. The number of languages included under the macrophylum, as reviewed above, speaks of its magnitude and the number of its speakers. It may, however, be noted that the above account is only to acquaint the reader with the major language phyla, and hence, is far from a detailed survey of the languages spoken in the continent of south America.

LANGUAGES IN MODERN INDIA

The people of modern India speak languages today, which belong to four distinct language families. These are: the *Austric*, the *Dravidian*, the *Tibeto-Chinese (Sino-Tibetan)*, and the *Indo-European*. The doyen of Indian linguists, Professor Suniti Kumar Chatterjee, has remarked in his book, *Languages and Literatures of India* (1963) that ancient India represented not only four language families, but four "language-culture" groups, affiliating each of the linguistic families to a specific culture group. Thus he justifies the mention of *Nishada, Dramida* or *Dravida, Kirata*, and the *Arya* in the ancient Sanskrit texts as the existence of these four language-culture groups from the ancient period of the Indian history.

I. Austric Languages in India

Austric family of languages has two subfamilies: (a) the Austro-Asiatic, and (b) the Austronesian. In India, we find the speakers of the Austro-Asiatic subfamily. The Austro-Asiatic subfamily is again divided into two branches: (a) Munda, and (b) Mon-Khmer. The Mon-Khmer speakers of India are confined to two groups; the Khasi of the Khasi and Jaintia Hills of Meghalaya, and the aboriginal Nicobarese of the Nicobar islands in the Bay of Bengal.

The Munda family spreads across a large number of tribal groups in central and eastern India, inhabiting the Chotanagpur plateau and Santal Pargana of Bihar, and the adjoining parts of Orissa, West Bengal and Assam. The main Munda branch of languages include, the Santali, Mundari, Bhumij, Birhor, Koda/Kora, Ho, Asuri, Birija/Birijia/Binjia, Korku, Kharia, Juang, Savara, Gadaba, and Kherwari. Among them, the Santali speakers outnumber the rest. The speakers of this group, according to Chatterjee, constituted the ancient group of Nishadas.

II. Sino-Tibetan Languages in India

The Sino-Tibetan family is again divided into two main subfamilies: (a) the Tibeto-Burman, and (b) the Siamese-Chinese. In India, we only find speakers of the Tibeto-Burman subfamily, who could be called as the ancient Kiratas. They are scattered over a large area, starting from Ladakh in the west to the State of Arunachal Pradesh in the northeast frontier and down to the southernmost tip of the State of Tripura. The Tibeto-Burman subfamily is further divided into three branches: (a) Tibeto-Himalayan, (b) North-Assam, and (c) Assam-Burmese.

The Tibeto-Himalayan branch has two main components. The Tibetan or Bhotia group consists of the Tibetan, Balti, Ladakhi, Lahuli, Sherpa and the Sikkim Bhotia. The Tibetan speakers are spread over Jammu and Kashmir, Punjab, Himachal Pradesh, Darjeeling district of West Bengal, and Arunachal Pradesh. The Balti and Ladakhi live in Jammu and Kashmir, while the Lahuli inhabit Punjab. The Sherpa have made Darjeeling their homeland, and the Bhotia live in Sikkim. The Himalayan group of the Tibeto-Himalayan branch consists of the Kanauri of Himachal Pradesh, and the Lepcha of Sikkim and Darjeeling.

The North-Assam or the Northeast Frontier branch is represented by the members of Aka, Dafla, Abor/Adi, Miri, Mishmi, and the Mishing communities of Arunachal Pradesh.

The Assam-Burmese branch is again divided into five groups: (a) Bodo, (b) Naga, (c) Kachin, (d) Kukichin, and (e) Burma. Each of these groups consists of a number of languages spoken by the people of Assam and the northeastern States of India, making it a real linguistic mosaic of India.

III. Dravidian Languages in India

The Dravidian language family in India is divided into three groups, based on the geographical area. These are: (a) south Dravidian, (b) central Dravidian, and (c) north Dravidian.

The south Dravidian group consists of Tamil, Malayalam, Kannada, Yerukula, Yerava, Kuruba/Kurumba, Coorgi, Tulu, Toda and Kota; their speakers being distributed in the southern part of the Deccan plateau.

The central Dravidian group is represented by Telugu, Kui, Kolami, Gondi, Parji, Koya, Khond/Kandh languages. The Telugu speakers obviously outnumber other groups, which are mostly tribals scattered over the States of Andhra Pradesh and the adjoining south Orissa.

Finally, the north Dravidian speakers are mainly distributed in the Chotanagpur area of Bihar, and adjoining Orissa and West Bengal, and are represented by the Kurukh/Oraon and Malto speakers.

It has been mentioned earlier, that another important Dravidian language, Brahui, is spoken in Baluchistan, far away from the Deccan plateau of India, and this has the highest concentration of Dravidian speakers. It is believed that Brahui is a remnant of the Dravidian language once spoken in Sind, Punjab and eastern Iran, having been pushed into the south of India with the Aryan invasion.

IV. Indo-European Languages in India

Indo-Aryan subfamily of the Indo-European family of languages has remained as the major subfamily in India. It is divided into three divisions : (a) the Eranian, (b) the Dardic, and (c) the Indo-Aryan. The Eranian branch of languages are spoken outside the boundary of India, and hence, we need not discuss it further here. One of the main Dardic languages is Kashmiri, spoken by the people of the State of Jammu and Kashmir.

The Indo-Aryan branch is further divided into six groups, which are spoken in many parts of India. (a) The North-Western Group includes Sindhi and Kachhi, spoken in Gujarat, Maharashtra, Rajasthan and Uttar Pradesh. (b) the Southern Group consists of Marathi and Konkani. While Marathi is spoken in Maharashtra. Konkani is spoken in Goa, Karnataka and Maharashtra. (c) The Eastern Group is represented by Oriya in Orissa, Bihari (Maithili, Magadhi and Bhojpuri varieties) in Bihar, Bengali in West Bengal, and Assamese in Assam. (d) The East-Central Group, consisting of Chhattisgarhi in Madhya Pradesh, Awadhi/Avadhi in U.P. and Bagheli, which are otherwise known as Eastern Hindi. (e) The Central Group is represented by Hindi (including Brijbhasa, Bundeli, Hindustsani and Kanauji) and spoken in the central and northern Indian states. Punjabi in Punjab, Rajasthani in Rajasthan, and Gujarati in Gujarat. (f) the Northern Group or the Himalayan Group is constituted by Nepali in West Bengal, Kumauni and Garhwali in U.P. and a group of Western Pahari (Jaunsari, Siramauri, Kului, Mandeali, Chameali, Gaddi, Churahi etc.), spoken in the Himalayan belt.

Since the publication of the *Linguistic Survey of India* by Grierson in 1903-28 (in 20 Volumes), many changes have taken place in the classification of Indian languages, on the basis of new research findings. The preceding survey is mostly based on the findings of Grierson and the modifications by Chatterjee. It does not deal with the details of all the languages, but presents a brief outline of major languages spoken in India.

9

APPLICATION OF ANTHROPOLOGICAL LINGUISTICS

A student of linguistic anthropology is often confronted with a common question from his colleagues with other specialisations is about the potential applications of his subject in the contemporary world. While the applications of social, cultural, and biological anthropology in the society have long been recognised, it is commonly assumed that anthropological linguistics has only a marginal application. But, in fact, the socially oriented linguistics or linguistic anthropology has many uses, which are being applied with increasing frequency to the problems having their roots in language use. Some of the widely recognised areas in which the knowledge of linguistic anthropology could be applied are, in the field of education to enhance literacy; in the fields of law, medicine, and business for more effective communication; and in the fields of language planning, language maintenance and language disorder (Salzmann, 1993:253).

ANTHROPOLOGY AND LANGUAGE PLANNING

One of the most practical uses of linguistic anthropology is in the field of language planning. Most societies in the contemporary world are multilingual or multi-dialectical for many historical and cultural reasons. In such a society, when several languages or dialects compete among themselves, language planning is necessary to assess the nature of the problem and to assign one of the competing languages the status of a national or an official language. Linguistic anthropologists, at this juncture, are the best specialists to advise, as they have first-hand information on the society and culture in question. This kind of decision is highly sensitive and requires reading of the problem most carefully, as it affects the entire population of the society. This very often follows the preparation of language policy, in writing of textbooks, grammars, dictionaries, and development of programmes for teachers' training, which a trained linguistic anthropologist can best handle.

What is described above, may be called two consecutive forms of language planning. The first involves a change in the status of a language or a dialect including its use, and the second involves the change in the structure of a language including pronunciation, spelling, grammar or vocabulary. While some language planning involve either of them, some need both, so that a new language emerges to cater to the needs of the people of the society. The nationalisation of Swahili and Hindi in Kenya and India respectively are the best examples of the change of the status of these languages in multi linguistic settings. In both Kenya and India, although English is one of the official languages, Swahili and Hindi have the privilege of being the national languages in their respective countries. As in Kenya, where Swahili is a lingua franca, in India, Hindi has become the lingua franca of a sort with its many local and regional variations. Despite some resentment in South India in having to accept Hindi as a lingua franca, the language is gradually becoming popular, thanks to the ever prospering Hindi film industry.

Language planning in India is still incomplete, taking into consideration the problem of a multitude of tribal languages and dialects in the country. Every tribe has its own language or dialect, and sometimes more than one. This creates problem in tribal education. When a tribal child goes to primary school, he has to speak, read and write many languages other than his own mother tongue, which most often does not have a script of its own. The tribal child has to learn the language of the state, the national language (Hindi), and of course, English at a later stage. Most of his teachers speak a language different from his mother tongue. This situation puts him at a disadvantage, and very often, he loses interest in going to the school. Tribal languages in India have not been developed, barring only a couple of them, although dictionaries of many tribal languages have been prepared by the British and other European linguists earlier. It is hoped that the expertise in linguistic anthropology might help to suggest ways and means to encourage and promote tribal languages, so that it would be no more an impediment in the area of tribal education in India.

The second kind of change, that involving change in the structure of a language has been witnessed in some countries, one being Turkey. When Turkey was Islamised in the 9th and 10th centuries, it adopted the Arabic script and borrowed many Arabic words. Later, when Persia became a part of the Turkish empire, the Turkish language borrowed many Persian words as well. As a result, at some point of time, original Turkish, Arabic and Persian words were available in Turkey for a single referent, which created a mesh of everything. In 1928, however, the Turkish President, Kemal Ataturk, appointed a commission to solve this problem, which recommended a Latin alphabet with several diacritics, which was ready to use in six weeks time. Gradually, planning was made to free Turkish from the Arabic and Persian loan words, which helped to modernise Turkish language and society (Salzmann, 1993: 263-264). In these efforts, where public cooperation goes along with linguistic planning and reformation, the expertise of a linguistic anthropologist is undoubtedly of use.

LANGUAGE MAINTENANCE

In many parts of the world, native languages are facing destruction, because of the state language policies, including in India. Michael Krauss considers that the coming century will see either the death or the doom of 90 per cent of human languages (1992 : 7). It is true that native languages spoken in Asia, Africa, Latin America, and even in the United States are facing severe threat from the dominant languages of the state or the region. In India, particularly, there is hardly any scope for the tribal languages to be maintained, improved and reinforced for the retention of the linguistic mosaic of the country. Due to the three-language formula for school children in India, tribal languages face extinction, despite efforts in some specific pockets to retain them. Example is Santali, spoken in Santal Pargana of Bihar and neighbouring West Bengal and Orissa. Pandit Raghunath Murmu, a Santali school teacher developed "Ol Chiki", a script for the language, and books and journals were published in that script. But it has not been followed up by suitable measures to further strengthen the linguistic base and formally introduce it in the schools. The case of Khamti in Arunachal Pradesh is another example of the extinction of the tribal language. The Khamti language has a script of its own, which is not the case in most other tribal languages in India. As Khamtis are Buddhists, even today, one finds their hand-written religious texts in Khamti scripts, preserved in many village monasteries. But there is no serious effort to develop and preserve the script. A few decades back, a section of the Khamti elite had given considerable attention to improvising the vocabulary and syntax in consultation with the Deccan College, Pune. But since another section of the Khamti elite considers it as a dead language, and show little interest in its improvement, the future of the language is not very promising (Misra, 1994). However, if the effort to teach Khamti language and script in primary schools continues, and if there is a political intervention to teach it in higher classes, as in the case of some of the American Indian languages, the language may yet survive.

The role of a linguistic anthropologist in such cases is very important. He has a very responsible role to play to convince the planning bodies for the retention and reinforcement of the tribal language and script, and motivate and guide the public effort to encourage essential improvements in the language to make it more acceptable.

Linguistic Anthropology in Law

The legal profession all over the world uses its own jargon, which is sometimes very difficult for even highly educated people to understand. The use of legal jargon at times becomes highly confusing for a lay man. For example, the simple expression of "Have an orange" might appear in legal language as : "I hereby give and convey to you, all and singular, my estate and interest, right, title, claim and advantages of and in said orange, together with its rind, skin, juice, pulp, and all rights and advantages therein and full power to bite, suck, or otherwise eat the same or give the same away with or without the rind, skin, juice, pulp and pips" (*The Tulsa Tribune* of October 6, 1959; quoted in Hager, 1959; quoted in Salzmann, 1993; 259). The use of legal jargon in court proceedings, therefore, directly affects the litigants themselves, the witnesses and the common man who tries to make some sense out of the court verdicts. Besides the court proceedings, the legal jargons in agreements and insurance policies become incomprehensible for the common user, and the role of a trained linguistic anthropologist in these situations to help in modifying the legal terms into simpler forms is of immense importance. In fact, more recently, insurance companies have started taking steps to write the policy documents in a more understandable language for policy holders, in consultation with the applied linguists or linguistic anthropologists.

The expertise of linguistic anthropologists is often sought in litigations relating to either the conflict between a spoken dialect and the instructional programme of a school (as described by Labov, 1982) or in cases of miscommunication between groups of speakers of different languages (see for example, Gumperz, 1982). The judges most often take note of the observations of the linguistic anthropologists in these special cases before making the final verdict. In legal cases involving communicative behaviour, usually the court likes to consider ". . . .the cultural background and communicative competence of the defendant, the plaintiff, and the witnesses; the types of questions asked during a trial (for example, the use of leading questions) and the context in which they are asked; the relative value of narrative testimony as against testimony limited to specific brief answers ; the use of interruptions; the relation between body movements and the utterances of litigants and witnesses; the nature of the instructions given by the jurors; and others". which proves beyond doubt that ". . . .linguistic expertise in court proceedings can be of value" (Salzmann, 1993: 262).

ANTHROPOLOGY AND LINGUISTIC RELATIVISM

Every anthropologist working among preliterate and simple societies encounters endangered language(s), as native languages face discrimination and extinction. The basic reason for this antipathy towards native languages is the elite notion that these languages are "inferior" and "primitive", compared to the dominant language(s) of the region. Native languages are often accused of being too simple and lacking in adequate vocabulary to name everything that others expect of them. In fact, linguists and anthropologists have already proved that all languages are equally complex, and sometimes native languages are rather more complex than the so-called developed languages. Secondly, the vocabulary of a language, as cognitive anthropologists have observed, depends upon "culturally significant" objects or materials. Brent Berlin's reference to 566 genera of plants in Aguaruna environmental knowledge in Peru, or Tyler's account of 8 varieties of bamboos easily recognisable by a Koya child, disproves the belief that native vocabulary is inadequate to comprehend the world. On the contrary, if Koya terminology does not have a term for spacecraft or chloroflurocarbon or surface-to-surface-misile, it does not reflect the inadequacy of the lexicon, such as the life experience of a Koya. The role here of a trained linguistic anthropologist is to help removing the misconception of the inadequacy of native languages by creating public awareness about these and related issues.

Another moral and ethical responsibility of an anthropologist working among preliterate and simple societies is to help them to improve their language by suggesting or helping to create scripts for the language, writing text-books in the native language for school children, neo and adult learners, improvising the grammar, enriching the lexicon etc. Since the anthropologist is closer to the native culture than others and is aware of their cultural and linguistic priorities and prescriptions, his role as a reformer of native languages has often the testimony of credibility and authenticity, which others should recognise and emulate. The anthropologist, therefore, has the responsibility to promote and preserve linguistic diversity in the world, and save the native languages from the threat of extinction.

BIBLIOGRAPHY

Aitchison, Jean (1983) *Linguistics* (second edition), Sevenoaks, Kent: Hodder and Stoughton.

Akmajian, A. *et al.* (1984) *Linguistics: An Introduction to Language and Communication* (second edition), Cambridge : The MIT Press.

Ardener, E. (ed) (1971) *Social Anthropology and Language*, London: Tavistock.

Bauman, Richard and Joel Sherzer (eds.) (1989) *Explorations in the Ethnography of Speaking* (second edition), London: Cambridge University Press.

Berlin, Brent (1976) "The Concept of Rank in Ethnobiological Classification: Some Evidence from Aguaruna Folk Botany", *American Anthropologist*, 3, 381-399.

Berlin, Brent and Paul Kay (1969) *Basic Color Terms: Their Universality and Evolution*, Berkeley: University of California Press.

Bloomfield, Leonard (1933) *Language*, New York: Holt.

Blount, Ben G. (1974) *Language, Culture and Society*, Cambridge, Mass.: Winthrop.

Boas, Franz (1911) "Introduction" in *The Handbook of American Indian Languages*, Bureau of American Ethnology, Bulletin 40, Washington: Government Printing Office.

Boas, Franz (1939) "A Report on the Committee on Research in American Native Languages, 1927-1937", *American Council of Learned Societies Bulletin*, No. 29.

Boas, Franz (1940) *Race, Language and Culture*, New York: Free Press.

Buettner-Janusch, J. (1973) *Physical Anthropology: A Perspective*, New York: Wiley.

Campbell, B.G.(ed)(1979) *Humankind Emerging* (second edition), Boston: Little, Brown.

Carrol, J.B. (1963) *The Study of Language*, Cambridge: Harvard University Press.

Casson, R. W. (ed) (1981) *Language, Culture and Cognitive: Anthropological Perspectives*, New York: Macmillan.

Chatterjee, S.K. (1963) *Languages and Literatures of India*, Calcutta: Bengal Publishers Pvt. Ltd.

Chomsky, Noam (1957) *Syntactic Structures*, The Hague: Mouton.

Chomsky, Noam (1972) *Language and Mind* (enlarged edition), New York: Harcourt Brace Jovanovich.

Conklin, Harold C. (1955) "Hanonóo Color Categories", *Southwestern Journal of Anthropology*, 11, 339-344.

Conklin, Harold C. (1959) "Linguistic Play in its Cultural Context", *Language*, 35, 631-636.

Crick, M. (1976) *Explorations in Language and Meaning: Toward a Semantic Anthropology*, London: Malaby Press.

Crystal, David (1991) *A Dictionary of Linguistics and Phonetics* (third edition), Cambridge: Cambrige University Press.

D'Andrade, Roy (1995) *The Development of Cognitive Anthropology*, Cambridge: Cambridge University Press.

Darlington, Cyril P. (1947) "The Genetic Component of Language", *Heredity, An International Journal of Genetics*, I, 269-286.

Darwin, Charles (1965) *The Expression of the Emotions in Man and Animals*, (reprint, original in 1872), London: University of Chicago Press.

DeSaussure, Ferdinand (1958) *Course in General Linguistics* (reprint, original in 1916), New York: Philosophical Library.

Dougherty, J.W.D. (ed) (1985) *Directions in Cognitive Anthropology*, Urbana and Chicago: University of Illinois Press.

Errington, J.J. (1988) *Structure and Style in Javanese: A Semiotic View of Linguistic Etiquette*, Philadelphia: University of Pennsylvania Press.

Evans-Pritchard, E.E. (1940) *The Nuer*, Oxford: Oxford University Press

Fasold, R.W. (1984) *Introduction to Sociolinguistics* (Vol I), New York: Blackwell.

Ferguson, C.A. (1959) "Diglossia", *Word,* 15, 325-340.

Fischer, J.L. (1958) "Social Influences in the Choice of a Linguistic Variant", *Word,* 14, 47-57.

Fishman, J.A. (ed.) (1968) *Readings in the Sociology of Language,* The Hague: Mouton.

Frake, C.O. (1961) "The Diagnosis of Disease among the Subanun of Mindanao", *American Anthropologist,* 63, 113-132.

Frake, C.O. (1964) "How to Ask for a Drink in Subanun", *American Anthropologist,* 66(6), 127-132.

Fromkin, Victoria and Rebert Rodman (1978) *An Introduction to Language* (second edition), New York Holt, Rinehart and Winston.

Gardner, R.A. and B.T. Gardner (1969) "Teaching Sign Language to a Chimpanzee", *Science,* 165, 664-672.

Giglioli, P.P. (ed.) (1972) *Language and Social Context: Selected Readings,* Baltimore: Penguin Books.

Gleason, H.A. Jr. (1961) *An Introduction to Descriptive Linguistics* (revised edition), New York: Holt, Rinehart and Winston.

Goodenough, W.H. (1957) "Cultural Anthropology and Linguistics", *Report of the Seventh Annual Round Table Meeting on Linguistics and Language Study* (Monograph No. 9) Washington: Georgetown University Press.

Greenberg, Joseph (1968) *Anthropological Linguistics,* New York: Random House.

Gudchinsky, S.C. (1956) "The ABC's of Lexicostatistics (Glottochronology)", *Word,* 12, 175-210.

Gumperz, J.J. (1964) "Linguistic and Social Interaction in two Communities", *American Anthropologist,* 66 (6), 137-153.

Gumperz, J.J. and Dell Hymes (eds.) (1972) *Directions in Sociolinguistics,* New York: Holt, Rinehart and Winston.

Hall, E.T. (1966) *The Hidden Dimension,* New York: Doubleday.

Hall, E.T. (1968) "Proxemics", *Current Anthropology,* IX, 83-108.

Hammond, P.B. (ed.) (1966) *Physical Anthropology and Archaeology,* New York: The Macmillan Company.

Harris, Marvin (1968) *The Rise of Anthropological Theory*, London: Routledge and Kegan Paul.

Hewes, G. (1976) "The Current Status of the Gestural Theory of Language Origins" in S. Harnad *et al.* (eds.) *Origins and Evolution of Language and Speech*, New York: Annals of the New York Academy of Science, Vol. 280.

Hickerson, N.P. (1980) *Linguistics Anthropology*, New York: Holt, Rinehart and Winston.

Hockett. C.F. (1958) *A Course in Modern Linguistics*, New York: Macmillan.

Hockett, C.F. (1973) *Man's Place in Nature*, New York: McGraw-Hill.

Hoebel, E.A. (1972) *Anthropology: The Study of Man*, New York: McGraw-Hill.

Hymes. Dell (ed.) (1964) *Language in Culture and Society*, New York: Harper & Row.

Hymes, Dell (1972) "Models of the Interaction of Language and Social Life" in J.J. Gumperz and Dell Hymes (eds.), *Directions in Sociolinguistics: The Ethnography of Communication*, 35-71, Philadelphia University of Pennsylvania Press.

Hymes, Dell (1974) *Reinventing Anthropology*, New York: Vintage Books.

Hymes, Dell (1983) *Essays in the History of Linguistic Anthropology* (Amsterdam Studies in the Theory and History of Linguistic Science, Vol. 25), Amsterdam and Philadelphia: Benjamins.

Jakobson, R. and Morris Halle (1956) *Fundamentals of Language*, The Hague: Mouton.

Jolly, Alison (1972) *The Evolution of Primate Behaviour*, New York: Methune.

Key, M.R. (1977) *Non-Verbal Communication: Research Guide and Bibliography*, Metuchen, NJ: Scarecrow Press.

Khubchandani, L.M. (1983) *Plural Languages, Plural Cultures: Communication, Identity, and Socio-political Change in Contemporary India*, Honolulu: University of Hawaii Press.

Kinkaid, M.D. *et al.* (eds.), (1975) *Linguistics and Anthropology*, Lisse : de Ridder Press.

Kluckhohn, Clyde (1949) *Mirror for Man : The Relation of Anthropology to Modern Life*, New York: McGraw-Hill.

Kramer, Cheris (1974) "Folk-linguistics: Wishy-washy Mommy Talk", *Psychology Today*, 8(1), 82-85.

Labov, William (1972) *Sociolinguistic Patterns*, Philadelphia: University of Pennsylvania Press.

Leach, E.R. (1974) *Lévi-Strauss* (revisededition), London: Fontana/Collins.

Lehmann, W.P. (1983) *Language: An Introduction*, New York: Random House.

Lenneberg, E.H. (1967) *Biological Foundations of Language*, New York: Wiley.

Lévi-Strauss, Claude (1963) *Structural Anthropology*, Harmondsworth: Penguin Books.

Lévi-Strauss, Claude (1966) *The Savage Mind*, Chicago : The University of Chicago Press.

Lieberman, Philip (1975) *On the Origins of Language*, New York: Macmillian.

Lieberman, Philip (1984) *The Biology and Evolution of Language*, Cambridge: Harvard University Press.

Luchsinger, R. (1940) "Die Sprache und Stimme von ein-und zweieiigen Zwillingen in Beziehungen zur Motorik und zum Erbcharakter", *Archiv der Julius Klaus Stiftung*, 15: 461-527.

Lyons, John (1978) *Noam Chomsky* (revised edition), New York Penguin Books.

Malinowski, Bronislaw (1922) *Argonauts of the Western Pacific*, London: Routledge.

Malinowski, Bronislaw (1926) *Myth in Primitive Psychology*, New York: Norton.

Mandelbaum, D.G. (ed.) (1949) *Selected Writings of Edward Sapir in Language, Culture, and Personality*, Berkeley: University of California Press.

Mazumdar, S.N. (1970) *Marxism and the Language Problem in India*, New Delhi: People's Publishing House.

Misra, K.K. (1994) *Tribal Elites and Social Transformation*, New Delhi: Inter-India.

Montagu, Ashley (1976) "Toolmaking, Hunting, and the Origin of Language" in S.N. Harnad *et al.* (eds.) *Annals of the New York*

Academy of Sciences (Vol. 280), 266-274, Honolulu: University of Hawaii Press.

Muhlhausler, Peter (1986) *Pidgin and Creole Linguistics*, Oxford: Blackwell.

Newman, Stanley (1955) "Vocabulary Levels: Zuni Sacred and Slang Usage", *Southwestern Journal of Anthropology*, 11, 345-354.

Ogden, C.K. and I.A. Richards (eds.) (1923) *The Meaning of Meaning*, New York: Harcourt.

Parker, Frank (1986) *Linguistics for Non-linguists*, Boston: Little, Brown.

Patterson, Francine (1978) "Conversations with a Gorilla", *National Geographic*, October.

Philips, Susan U. *et al.* (eds.) (1987) *Language, Gender, and Sex in Comparative Perspective*, Cambrige, Cambridge University Press.

Philipsen, Gerry and Donal Carbaugh (1986) "A Bibliography of Fieldwork in the Ethnography of Communication", *Language in Society*, 15, 387-397.

Pike, Kenneth L. (1967) *Language in Relation to a Unified Theory of Structure of Human Behaviour* (second revised edition), The Hague : Mouton.

Premack, Ann James and David Premack (1972) "Teaching Language to an Ape", *Scientific American*, 227, 4, 92-99.

Pride, J.B. and Janet Holmes (eds.) (1972) *Sociolinguistics : Selected Readings*, New York : Penguin Books.

Robins, R.H. (1967) A Short History of Linguistics, London: Longmans, Green and Co Ltd.

Roitblat, H.L. *et al.* (eds.) (1992) *Language and Communication: Comparative Perspectives*, Hillsdale, NJ: Eelbaum.

Salzmann, Zdenek (1993) *Language, Culture, Society: An Introduction to Linguistic Anthropology*, Boulder: Westview Press.

Samovar, Larry A. and R.E. Porter (eds.) (1991) *Intercultural Communication: A Reader* (sixth edition), Belmont, CA: Wadsworth.

Sampson, Geoffrey (1980) *Schools of Linguistics: Competition and Evolution*, London: Hutchinson.

Sapir, Edward (1921) *Language: An Introduction to the Study of Speech*, New York: Harcourt, Brace.

Sapir, Edward (1929) "The Status of Linguistics as a Science" *Language*, 5, 207-214.

Saville-Troike, Muriel (1989) *The Ethnography of Communication: An Introduction* (second edition), Oxford: Blackwell.

Sebeok, T.A. (ed) (1977) *How Animals Communicate*, Bloomington: Indiana University Press.

Simpson, George G. (1969) *Biology and Man*, New York: Harcourt.

Simpson, J.M.Y. (1969) *A First Course in Linguistics*, Edinburgh: The University Press.

Stoss, Brian (1976) *The Origin and Evolution of Language*, Dubuque, Iowa: W.C. Brown.

Sturtevant, W.C. (1964) "Studies in Ethnoscience", *American Anthropologist*, 66 (1), 99-131.

Swadesh, Morris (1950) "Salish Internal Relationships", *International Journal of American Linguistics*, 16: 157-167.

Swadesh Morris (1971) *The Origin and Diversification of Languages*, Chicago: Aldine.

Tarnoczy, T.H. (1947) "Physical Characteristics of speech Sounds and Some Aspects of their Anthropological Relations", *Acta Anthropobiologica* (Budapest), I: 1-43.

Tedlock, Dennis (1983) *The Spoken Word and the Work of Interpretation*, Philadelphia: University of Pennsylvania Press.

Thorne, Barrie *et al.* (eds.) (1983) *Language, Gender, and Society*, Rowley, MA: Newbury House.

Todd. Loreto (1993) *An Introduction to Linguistics* (5th impression), Harlow, Essex: Longman York Press.

Trager, George L. (1972) *Language and Languages*, San Francisco: Chandler.

Trudgill, Peter (ed.) (1974) *Applied Sociolinguistics*, Orlando : Academic Press.

Tyler, S.A. (ed.) (1969) *Cognitive Anthropology*, New York: Holt, Rinehart and Winston, Inc.

Voegelin, C.F. and F.M. Voegelin (1957) *Hopi Domains*, Bloomington, Ind: Indiana University Publications in Anthropology and Linguistics Memoir 14.

Voegelin, C.F. and F.M. Voegelin (eds) (1964-1966) " Languages of the World" *Anthropological Linguistics*, 6-8.

Wardhaugh, Ronald (1986) *An Introduction to Sociolinguistics*, New York: Blackwell.

Washburn, S.L. and I. DeVore (1961) " The Social Life of Baboons", *Scientific American*, June.

Waterman, J.T. (1970) *Perspectives in Linguistics*, Chicago: The University of Chicogo Press.

Weitz, Shirley (ed.) (1979) *Nonverbal Communication* (Second Edition), New York: Oxford University Press.

Whorf, Benjamin L. (1940a) "Science and Linguistics" *Technology Review*, 42, 229-231; 247-248.

Whorf, Benjamin L. (1940b) "Linguistics as an Exact Science", *Technology Review*, 43, 61-63; 80-83.

Whorf, Benjamin L. (1956) *Language, Thought and Reality: The Selected Writings of Benjamin Lee Whorf*, Cambridge, Mass: The M.I.T. Press.

Witherspoon, Gary (1977) *Language and Art in the Navajo Universe*, Ann Arbor, Mich: University of Michigan Press.

Woolford Ellen B. (1979) "Aspects of Tok Pisin Grammar", *Pacific Linguistics*, Series-B, Monograph No. 66, Canberra: Australian National University.

Yule, George (1996) *The Study of Language* (second edition), Cambridge: Cambridge University Press.

INDEX